"LCFC" 1.5: The Fall Memoir

By: Kevin Anglade

LOWERED CONCRETE

"Life Comes From Concrete" 1.5

By: Kevin Anglade

Contents

Nice Guys Finish Last

The Reality = Life Is Real!

Generations

Family

Georges Anglade

Thank you for shaping and molding me into a man. My only regret is us not getting the chance to bond more as father and son. Nonetheless, I carry you in my heart each and every day. I love you.

Acknowledgements

First and foremost, I would like to thank God for always guiding and protecting me throughout all of my steps. My mother for being strong and beautiful. My sister Samantha. Flowered Concrete. Tupac for his book of poems called *The Rose That Grew From Concrete* as it was an integral part to the creation and inspiration behind this book. I also want to thank him for the spark and rise of Flowered Concrete as a publishing company. Mia Hill for being my biggest cheerleader, supporter, best friend and confidant. Roy Diaz for photography. Divin Mathew for additional photography. Tai Allen for being a great mentor. Shola Gbemi for documenting his experiences. Max Desmarais for inserting his time capsule to inscribe his story. Bertrand St. Jean and Robert Antequera Jr. for providing me with concepts for "Destiny" and "Life Is Real!" And last, but not least, Emir Fils-Aime, for his insight, depth and intellect concerning this project and as a fellow artist serving their purpose. Thank you all.

Foreword: Max's Journey

My name is Dautchley Desmarais and I am twenty-two-years-old. I was once placed in foster care at the age of eleven. During my time spent within the system, I kept moving from house to house because I wasn't getting treated fairly and sometimes I just refused to follow the rules.

When attending school, I never had the latest clothes or sneakers such as Air Jordans and because of this, the other kids would often tease me. After a while, I didn't want to go to school because whenever I went, kids would call me a dirty bum and degrade me however they saw fit due to my fashion choices or lack thereof. Some things I clearly remember being made fun of were my teeth and nappy hair. As a result, it made me feel really insecure.

Naturally, I got into a lot of fights because I didn't get along with others because of how they treated me. This then led to my habit of skipping class, which gradually increased over time until one day I finally stopped attending altogether.

Since school was no longer a part of my daily activities, I often found myself in Canarsie, where my friends and I would rob cars that weren't secured and took any and everything left inside. One day in particular as our momentum picked up, I remember us getting caught by an off-duty female cop that promised to shoot us for our juvenile ways. That was a real crucial moment for me to experience as I slowed down in that department.

As for foster care, when I ended up in the system, I was often depressed and instead of progressing, it made me worse. Moreover, I didn't have enough to eat as most of the foster mothers that took me in used my presence as a means to receive a check.

This time period was really hard on my biological mother. She was often stressed and upset with me because she was trying to raise me right. Yet, I was just too troublesome and often did the opposite of what I was supposed to be doing. As a result, my problematic nature led to me bouncing around from home to home. It was very difficult, as I had no structure and foundation within my life.

It was something I wanted, something I felt I had never had, and something I yearned for. There was a void that definitely needed to be filled, so in order to immerse myself into a "family" of some sorts, I decided to join a gang.

Living in Brownsville at the time, most of my friends were selling drugs and were making a lot of money. Their tendency to make fast cash enabled them to get a lot of girls. And so, me seeing the results of their hustle and spirit out on that corner, unsurprisingly, I wanted to be a part of it. Although, being in a gang only made me an easy target because since I'm a bit on the short side, people would always test my toughness.

What sparked my change of pace and eventual change was a woman that was my advisor since my freshman year in high school, named Una Karim.

Una saw that I was heading for failure and to prevent it, she did all that she possibly could to point me in the right direction towards success. For starters, she had me sign up for a photography program in Harlem called "Expanding The Walls", and from that point on, my whole life changed.

I remember instantly falling in love with art when I sold a picture I took called "Fly Runners" for a hundred dollars. The result of this blew me away as I was so used to being in the streets and selling drugs. Never in a millions years would I have thought that a young brother from the hood could make such kind of money by doing something positive (and artistic). For me, the only way I knew how to make money was by being in the streets and doing negative things. As a result, the experience was a defining moment for me at the time.

Throughout my stint within the program, I still wasn't really focused or interested in attending school, however, Una never gave up on me. I can recall her writing me on Facebook one day and asking me: "Is the street life something you really want or do you want something better?" After reading her message, I thought about it and decided it was really time for me to take school seriously. Thus, after several months of missing so many classes I went back to school.

At first, it was a struggle to finish but I was relentless as I kept pushing myself to do the work even when I felt like quitting. Eventually, I finished and ended up graduating as I received my high school diploma. The accomplishment was bitter-sweet because by Una writing me on Facebook and telling me to get my life together, it made me realize that there were people that really cared about me and it wouldn't have been right if I kept ignoring their great intentions by hurting myself.

As mentioned before, Una could have given up on me like most people. And up until her intervention, I honestly can admit that I had given up on myself. Throughout this early portion of my life journey, I'm starting to realize that everything I have been through and all of the people I've come across in both negative and positive circumstances made me move smarter and has enabled me to have a closer relationship with God.

An example of this was when I was heading home one day and I met two beautiful souls performing poetry on the C train. Their poetry instantly captivated me as I was moved by their words, passion, and spirit. Because of it, I felt as if they were speaking directly to me and asked them for their contact information. This was yet another instant of my life changing on the spot. In my initial exchange of words with them, one of those beautiful souls (whose name was Toya) invited me to my first open mic in Brownsville. After experiencing it, I started writing and performing. This has done nothing but wonders for me as a human being because I finally have something to believe in. For once, I finally have some hope.

After my verbal exchange with those two poets, a lady on that same exact train told me to never forget where I come from. Since then, I have started going to more open mics and connecting with other beautiful souls.

On Thanksgiving Day in 2015, I met Kevin Anglade, an author and poet through a mutual friend named Joshua Walker who was having a Thanksgiving Day holiday giveback in Bedford-Stuyvesant. The giveback featured an array of talent as poets, rappers and singers performed while volunteers and organizations simultaneously distributed food and clothes to the homeless. After speaking with Kevin, I was truly amazed at his endeavors and found out that he had started his own publishing company called Flowered Concrete. He in turn was impressed by my words and spirit and told me a bit about what he does as the founder and president of the company. After getting my feet wet in writing, a goal of mine has always been to publish a poetry book like my idol Tupac and it just so happens that I am on a quest to get it done. After that, who knows where it will take me?

One thing I am certain of nonetheless is that my mother is proud of me and of the changes I've made as a young man and as a person overall. Going forward, I will soon be a published author and once

I become one, you will then experience my story as I am *The Flower after the Storm.*

Peace & Love,

Dautchley "Max" Desmarais

"This Is Temporary"

Foster care

 Got me here

The pain & the struggle

Got me here

The grind & the hustle

 Got me here

It's better from where I was

It's still not fair

But what I'm going through now

Will get me there

Part I: Life is Concrete

I was born on January 21st, 1991 at the Brooklyn Hospital Center approximately around 11pm. My mother has told me on numerous occasions that I was a reserved baby. She would always tell me,

"You? You never made any noise as an infant, but your sister? Forget about it!"

My sister that she speaks of happens to be my younger sibling, Samantha.

Located on the west side of Fort Greene Park, the hospital happens to be the oldest within the borough of Brooklyn. As a kid, I always heard that my mother couldn't take me home the day that I was born due to a bad cold I caught within my first few hours of existence. Therefore, I stayed in the hospital for several weeks until my infection subsided and I was allowed to be taken home. Being that I was born on January 21st, my birthday fell on a Monday, Martin Luther King Jr.'s birthday to be exact. As I'm writing this, I'm finding it to be really special as well as an honor to have been born on such a day.

"Concrete"

I used to dream every night[i]

Now when I do its rare[ii]

I hope its cause my social rank is climbing up the stairs[iii]

Remember seeing kids with toys and wanted what was theirs

And now this life is just a breeze

The wind is blowing in my hair

Grandma used to care for me

My parents went to work

They didn't want to see their little son become a jerk

Brooklyn, Notorious, Criminals[iv]

This is no subliminal

The chances are I could have gone biserk

Many people see my life and think that it is glory

But truth is they don't know the half of my story

Everything I ever have attained

Or I've gained is only because I went

and snatched the things that weren't for me

Let me take you back awhile, 1997

A six-year-old with innocence you'd think I was in heaven[v]

Fire started in my house, my family put it out, no doubt

We had escaped just when we should have went to heaven [vi]

Now the year 2007 really could have been cruel

It was August; a hiatus

I was definitely outta school

In Georgia for the summer with my momma and my sis

When I sank into the deep, almost lifeless in a pool[vii]

And lifeless I'd become upon the day I lost my sister[viii]

And up until this day without a doubt you know I miss her

Sixteen at the time but I was forced to mature

Becoming something else that I wasn't when I was with her

Three years pass and so my Dad is now gone

Remember thinking to myself that life "is all wrong"[ix]

It was Jamaica Hospital where he told me to go home

The last to ever see him damn, where do I belong?[x]

Hopefully the last time of something so rash

But April 24th I suffered through a car crash[xi]

With me and my sister Sam inside on a ride[xii]

Back to Queens as is it spun, and so I thought we'd surely die[xiii]

I hope that you don't pity me as I write this

Like when I thought I was a goner due to hepatitis[xiv]

Now all it does is ignite us, no doubt that we can fight this[xv]

Live to fight another day is better than "just lifeless"[xvi]

We are priceless, I'm just glad that I've been living it righteous[xvii]

Block out the negatives, there's absolutely nothing you can't do[xviii]

I self-published my very first book at twenty-two

I mean damn who woulda knew?

Be you and not Blue[xix]

Don't allow any hater to rightfully guess at all your clues[xx]

I hope you understand with my flow

That I know how I rose

From the concrete, it's where we all grow[xxi]

"My Words Are Like A River..."

I started writing poetry in the spring of 2012 after finishing my first semester at Brooklyn College as a transfer student.

I decided to begin writing poems as a way to express myself. Also, during that time, I stumbled across Tupac's book of poetry titled *The Rose That Grew From Concrete* and let me tell you something, after reading that book, I swiftly became enamored with the art form.

Prior to reading the collection, I was never a big fan of poetry or poems in general; but the way Tupac wrote poetry, it had purpose, it had meaning, and most importantly, it had rhythm. Therefore, I wasted no time in crafting and constructing poems of my own. To this day, I vividly remember the first poem I wrote. It went a little something like this:

"Land of the free, there's no time to backtrack, so pray that you're saved by the bells, like Zack. Yes I'm hot, turn on the A.C. Slater, I'm just repaying society, four hundred years of labor."

Although it was littered with pop culture references from the 1990's NBC teenage sitcom *Saved By The Bell,* I now see that there was actually some dope rawness to what I wrote. The fact that I wrote about repaying society after 400 years of systematic oppression, it showed that from the get go I always wanted to talk about something of importance as well as shed light, knowledge, and positivity unto a new generation.

"Conscious"

Never liked AKA's[xxii]

Call me just by my name

It's Kev with a heart and a plea I feel your pain[xxiii]

Achieved and more to do, just meant for me to gain

I'm a 3.5 Wu-Tang among your brain[xxiv]

No money to feed the city

No money to feed the poor

I rack for ten years; money for me to war[xxv]

I said there's more to do, I'm only gonna get better

So Jerry avoids the traps he only comes out for cheddar[xxvi]

You're in just for the money and in it just for the fame

Shout out to Tom and Jerry [xxvii]

I just middled my name[xxviii]

My list is full of dreams, Coolio, I dread[xxix]

If you didn't get that I went over your head

The streets won't stop to get you

Take care, It makes me quiver

Kids die in Brownsville; Cirrhosis; The Liver[xxx]

You lose a loved one, things never remain the same

This game called life where we laugh, we pain

Life can be a bitch so I don't suggest we trust her[xxxi]

I lead the new school so you can just call me Busta[xxxii]

Rhyming is a passion of mine, I'm ill at it[xxxiii]

I knowledge you and auto the truth, I'm Illmatic[xxxiv]

My words are like a river no need to speak em' I flow em' [xxxv]

I flow my words and serve em' so you can just say I poem[xxxvi]

"Bits of Inspiration"

SEGA is inspired by a poem that can be found within Tupac Shakur's *The Rose That Grew From Concrete* called "Only 4 the Righteous" where Pac utilizes an old-school, divine rap flow that completely exhibited his boisterous presence as an MC.

In that poem, he would write a word that best described him as a rapper at the starting margin of each line and would briefly elaborate upon it with smooth debonair and flash.

Upon my first initial reading of the poem, I can remember being so moved by the rhythm and precision of each line that it inspired me to create a modern day version of my own that I felt represented me as the twenty-one-year-old young man I had become at the time.

When performed or read, the poem sounds fun and in many ways it is! However, although it may appear as something kid-friendly with inspiring and uplifting overtones, it never shies away from its serious and introspective undertones.

I remember writing this one in my local library at Baisley Park, a library that I had been going to for years and still do whenever I feel the need to be humbled by a sense of community.

At the age of twenty-one, I wouldn't say that I had my life figured out, but at the same time, I understood my sense of purpose. I understood that I had a lot of things that I had to take care of as a result of the passing of my father and the financial hardships that my mother was left to face. After witnessing my mother become a widow and single parent, I knew that I had no time for fun and games as I was left to become a man in my own right.

Those are some of the topics that I loosely tackle in the poem. My father, (God rest his soul) had sacrificed so much in order to raise my sister and I. He had left his country of origin (Haiti) in the late seventies just to increase his quality of life and upon reconvening with my mom, spontaneously at a grocery store in Brooklyn, (they grew up together) I would later be brought into the fold.

I can honestly say, and you might hear me repeat it many times within this book and upon seeing me in person that if it wasn't for my Dad and all of his teachings, I wouldn't be who I am today. Therefore, if there is anything that I can truly say about my father that resonates with me even now, is that he always wanted my sister Samantha and I to become something in life. It's funny because as I write this, I can still hear my father telling me in his all-too-familiar booming deep voice, "Kevin, stay straight!" (meaning keep a righteous and wholesome path) And straight I remain as I never get caught up into what my peers are doing but more so with what I must do to succeed as an individual.

"SEGA"

16 bits like SEGA, a few years out of my teens[xxxvii]

"Kings?" Conceived in that county but bred in Queens[xxxviii]

"Queens?" Yes, sometimes forgotten but still the greatest[xxxix]

"Greatest" and life is a game, so I play it[xl]

"Play" Press start on the deck to start my day[xli]

"Day" refreshing young black men in every way[xlii]

"Way" In life there's two options good or bad[xliii]

"Bad" never that, I wanna be like my Dad

"Dad" Is gone, so I now look up to his brother[xliv]

"Man?" Yes I am, just taking care of my mother[xlv]

And "Sister, Sister" Oh tell me how did I miss her?[xlvi]

Without her there is pain just call me another blister[xlvii]

"Special" I am not, so come to the realization

"Example" My actions are leading a generation[xlviii]

"Current" Events, constant changes just like the weather [xlix]

"Late" I never am, unifying people together[l]

"Dreams within a Gallery"

I remember kicking it with one of my boys named Bert who stayed over at my place for the 2012 holiday season. During that time frame, I remember spitting a lot of my poetry to him just so he could see my progression as a young man and where I was artistically trying to go. Bert, whose personality was bright, animated and vibrant, said to me,

"Yo Kev, son. I can see you writing or recording something I've got in my head."

"What is it?" I then asked him.

Bert who was seated upon a stool within my kitchen yelled enthusiastically, "I know a girl named Destiny, she's looking like my Destiny…Destiny…Destiny!"

I then responded and told him,

"Yo, that is dope, I definitely gotta do something with that."

However, I placed it in the back of my mind until one day I was sitting at home, the following month in January and it came to me. Without any hesitation, I started jotting down the words as fast as they had come into my Blackberry phone.

The reason why I like "Destiny" and didn't think twice about including it within this book is because I've always been a person searching for his sole purpose; a person who is immersed upon the search of his destiny and aspiring to achieve greatness.

"Destiny"

I know a girl named Destiny she's lookin' like my Destiny[li]

I think it's safe to say that she's in the world that's meant for me

What's great about her is that she was never truly left for me

But moved me and my pen like a future in tune that's meant for me

Destiny, Destiny I truly believe

that with you by my side there is nothing I won't achieve

You'll always calm my stress in the cab like Aleve[lii]

You tell me time and time again, always believe

That anything is possible gotta be done to do it

Support me every day when I tell you I will pursue it

My dreams will never falter cause you will decide to sue it[liii]

You said that you would hold me like Elmer would do to glue it[liv]

I tell you each and every day that I will go and chase it

The future's round the corner and I'm not too far to taste it

I told you that it's coming so I ain't gon' have to race it[lv]

Cause sooner than a later work ethic will have to face it[lvi]

Destiny, Destiny, do you know that I'm coming?

A thief within the night or a ticket just like a summons [lvii]

Or a marching band as them sticks just consist to drummin'

Like a Jordan brand it will never do cease the dummin'[lviii]

Man I need you bad like those gangstas in Heat and drama[lix]

And the U.S. lads when they Bin had looked for Osama[lx]

Seven figure numerals breaking within some commas

I need to save the world I'm talking about my mama[lxi]

Destiny, Destiny, you know just what I want

Until I reach my goal it is only you that I'll haunt

But don't you ever think you will ever be what I taunt

I need you by my side for people to see I flaunt

Within my reach you're not that far in actuality

You're more real than a TV and all its realities

Can't wait for all your benefits, call it a salary

I'm writing up my destiny deep in this gallery[lxii]

"Life Isn't What It Seems"

Out of all the poems that I have been blessed to write so far in my young life, I can indubitably say that this one resonates with me the hardest.

First and foremost, we've all heard the saying "nothing is promised" but in truth, until we've actually experienced something being taken away from us, we can never truly understand it.

I can certainly say that I'm a living advocate of the theory as I've had my fair share of brushes with death or have experienced the losses of loved ones. This poem came to me not long after a time where I had to experience such heartache in losing someone deeply close to me and in whom I truly loved.

After receiving a phone call late in the evening on July 18th, 2013 at approximately 11pm, I couldn't believe that I had lost someone within a blink of an eye and without warning. Her name was Bianca Leigh Petillo, she was an eighteen-year-old girl who attended my church and who I pretty much grew up with. Her death affected me so hard that not long after, I soon began to question my existence and would internally ask, "what is the point of life when you only get screwed over in the end?"

Up until that time I had spontaneously lost my eldest sister, father, maternal grandmother and then Bianca. I just couldn't understand it at all. It reminded me that on any given day or any given moment you could be as good as gone.

From that point forward, I wondered for the rest of the summer if I would ever achieve the goals and dreams that I had often aspired to attain. It made me utterly paranoid to the point where I briefly lost the joy in living. But after coming to terms that it had all been God's plan, there was nothing left for me to worry about. God had wanted Bianca for his heavenly kingdom and in that moment, he brought her back to her rightful home.

Later on, I finally realized that instead of continuously moping and mourning in her memory, and in that of my father and in that of my sister, it was time that I finally lived. Without further questioning their sudden departures, I took the experiences as a lesson learned and wrote down my fears and thoughts. And with this poem, I think I fully expressed all of the tension, paranoia and pent-up anxieties that had been building within me during that difficult time.

"Thirty?"

Things have happened in my life

Some good, some bad, it irks me

I'm often left to ask God will I live to see age thirty?[lxiii]

I hope he sees me worthy so new state of mind like Jersey

My sister ceased at twenty-six her absence it still hurts me

It's crazy, crazy, crazy, how life can become a maybe[lxiv]

Was stable the other day 'til I received word I had lost my baby[lxv]

I'm thinking life is shady and maybe it's trying to play me[lxvi]

That's why as human beings you only go by the day see?[lxvii]

Cause if I could predict the future

There were many things I would have stalled

I would have told my Daddy to quit and that he's dying of alcohol

I heard that he had a fall it was the last time that he was tall[lxviii]

My girl would have never died would have been prevented by just a call[lxix]

But let me tell you something I'm doing all that I can

To live my life with courage just trying to be a man

Daddy was replaced the moment he hit the can

Before he left the earth he knew that I was the man

And living out your daily life isn't just what it seems

The world's just one big gamble can't promise all of your dreams[lxx]

Shooting for the long haul while counting all of its seams[lxxi]

You live and die and that's the truth [lxxii]

A basket of these things[lxxiii]

Now I'm counting all my days just seeing where I can take it[lxxiv]

I want to be like "eighty-three" hopefully I'll make it

And nope, I won't forsake it, I really just gotta make it

Cause if I died today, you think my momma could take it?

In thirty-five months she lost her husband and oldest daughter

I watched just like a witness the tears that it had brought her

That's why I'm living smarter my ambitions are even harder

But if I do die violent like Hampton I am a Martyr[lxxv]

Cause my lyrics, I seer it, America will even fear it[lxxvi]

My fellow brothers revere it, the FBI will leer it[lxxvii]

Which leads me on to rear it, cause FEDS can't even bear it[lxxviii]

My bed they then get near it, my head is gone, they teared it[lxxix]

Although I'm sure this life will never be what it seems

At least let me see thirty, I gotta achieve my dreams

Part II: NICE GUYS FINISH LAST

"Kristina"

I've been thinking about you lately and I don't know why

Deep down to be honest, I once broke down and cried[lxxx]

And so I'm heaving out some sighs, our relationship was a lie

Am I wrong for saying that I possibly want to die?

Let me go back and retract, I'm a real sensitive guy

But that's truly how I felt on whichever day you left me[lxxxi]

I would have gave you my all, but listen girl you wouldn't let me

I'm gloomy like the day you met me and that was the sign[lxxxii]

That all that glitters isn't gold, you just didn't come debt free[lxxxiii]

When I was with you I was truly lost[lxxxiv]

I dropped everything at all costs

But my sister, I truly lost[lxxxv]

For you? Her, I tossed

But now everything's repaired[lxxxvi]

Except this big despair

It's like I'm pulling out my hair

And you cut me off like nair[lxxxvii]

So now I'm asking: "did you care?"

My love was real and rare

This pain I just can't bear

And life just isn't fair

Cause your my past, so no more sound[lxxxviii]

I'm back girl, like rebound[lxxxix]

And I was your rebound[xc]

Your pitcher had left the mound [xci]

He then wanted to hound

Your love for which I found

To him you're always bound[xcii]

Our love then went way down

But seriously, he's just a clown

Your prom, I did calm down[xciii]

A night I should have known

Cause later you couldn't be found

You know, twas all a swirl[xciv]

The way our *"love"* unfurled[xcv]

And now it makes me hurl

Can't penalize my new girl[xcvi]

But all the same, just different day[xcvii]

With her, pain just fades away[xcviii]

And I'm glad she's here to stay

She says the route's one way [xcix]

And I always head your way

Summer days, every Tuesday[c]

Bethel Gospel from where I pray[ci]

Where it keeps me from going gray[cii]

Wishing you the best of luck

For the next guy; yeah man, good luck

No stability, she runs a muck

Just hope, she stays a buck [ciii]

"Feelings"

When exactly?[civ]

I never knew[cv]

I only thought

I'd care for you

Sounds familiar

A worldwide tour[cvi]

Expressed my thoughts

You shut the door

Just a dream[cvii]

Stuck in the past [cviii]

I took my time

It wasn't fast

Replaced love for rules[cix]

I tried to bend

I think it messed

With us as friends

Surprised myself

You grew appealing

I was surely

catching feelings

"Something?"

You congratulated me on my achievements[cx]

But on the real, I've accomplished nothing

You said you miss me and my sister

But in my mind, I think you're bluffing

These inner thoughts are muffling

Your words hold weight like stuffing [cxi]

I just know the well runs deep[cxii]

So please tell me, do you still feel something?

Truth is, unto this day

Believe me, I really do miss you

And believe it or not, every day

I still wish to be with you

Although I long to kiss you

He's there and that's the issue

I pray each day of your life is love

That's real, no box of tissue[cxiii]

But if it doesn't you must acquit[cxiv]

Just maybe a false glove

We're all searching for love

That is pure like white dove[cxv]

So I'll be waiting for mine[cxvi]

Word to the man whose up above

Signed yours truly and sincerely

From Jerry, it will always be love[cxvii]

"Black Girl"

One of the first true creations of this world

I'm talking about you specifically black girl

You're precious like sixty minutes within an hour

We all know that you come from a higher power

You are truly one of God's greatest conceptions

You are beauty and I love your perception

And yes you talk a lot and are sometimes mental[cxviii]

But you always speak your mind

Girl, you're loving, kind, and gentle

So remember black girl to always

Carry and conduct yourself like a lady[cxix]

And when you do, find a gentleman

Just as my mother did **who raised me**[cxx]

"Bianca"

Everything was going smooth upon that weird
Thursday [cxxi]

When James had called within the night I had to
stop 2K[cxxii]

And then I thought about my day at the library
with pen[cxxiii]

Just writing up my second book for all my fiction
friends[cxxiv]

But as I wrote, my feelings felt straight rotten to the
core

At 6:14 I never thought I'd write just
anymore[cxxv]

All of us here that are struck on earth are truly sad
and miss you

And as for me? Well I'm just glad I had the chance
to kiss you

Did I mention that I miss you?

You know, I really do wish to

See you again, in the flesh, but knowing I can't is
really the issue

I once said that your interest in me

Was very consistent and bold[cxxvi]

And that I'd say led for our love to blossom and unfold

Persistence truly built and sold[cxxvii]

Your love for me like gold

We tried and tried but our result: a story that didn't unfold[cxxviii]

Too mature?[cxxix]

I guess…maybe

A few years apart?[cxxx]

It didn't phase me[cxxxi]

Although you knew we shared these jokes

"What If" about our baby?[cxxxii]

All of us that still remain are trying to stay strong[cxxxiii]

Including all of your siblings that are sulking all day long[cxxxiv]

Josh is in a funk you see?

While Britt is feeling guilty

Myles is really never home

And all my thoughts are milky[cxxxv]

Last week at mass I sat and watched

Your mom break down and cry[cxxxvi]

Man, I knew I felt it too

Cause love defeats the pride[cxxxvii]

I messaged Myles at work today[cxxxviii]

My words were meant sincerely[cxxxix]

His Iphone was in hand Sunday, a pic of you was near me[cxl]

Of you I stop to think

Because my heart pours out like sink[cxli]

You see this is life is far from pink[cxlii]

And I'm just caught between the brink[cxliii]

Therefore, as sure as words, as sure as death

When it rains, oh yes, it pours[cxliv]

The only girl who stole my heart[cxlv]

For you I write this for…

PART III:

THE REALITY=LIFE IS REAL...

"Divided by Greed"

   Although the following poem happens to be the first of this particular section of the book, it actually is one of the last poems I wrote in preparation for this project.

   When I wrote this actual piece, I wanted to write about the daily struggles I've witnessed personally or have heard by ear in New York City. Often more times than not, New York gets bigged up for being one of the greatest cities in the world; and rightfully so, it certainly is. However, for every Union Square or SoHo, there is a homeless man on the corner just trying to get by. For every *"Lion King"* on Broadway in Time Square, there is a woman starving and who hasn't eaten in days. For every child of color who may be going about his or her business, whether it's coming home from school or playing basketball with friends, there is a cop who stops and frisks just because he or she may believe that the child is up to no good. These are just some of the things that happen daily within the five boroughs or any city with a vast discrepancy between the majority and the minority as well as the rich and the poor.

While I certainly have a strong passion and love for New York City, I also know that the politics of it are messed up and that the people deserve better than what they've been given.

The reason this poem stands out in my mind more than any of the others poems is because I wrote it down on paper. Well, at least its first draft anyway. As for my other poems, I found that pen and paper didn't work out for the few pieces that I tried to write down and so, I usually write them into my BlackBerry phone.

As you read "New York", you will get the chance to see me play around with the many contradictions that occur within the city every day. Also, you will read the metaphors and hear the onomatopoeia's that will enable you to paint a picture of what a true New Yorker sees while living in such a tourist attraction environment.

"New York"

I'm living in a state of mind

A mental state of mine

You see what makes and breaks my state of mind

Is New York state of mind

It is a place where poor don't eat

It is a place where law has crumbled

It is a place where niggas see themselves

Trapped within a jungle

I call the state, my place, my home

Which means I am a purist [cxlvi]

So all is sweet and neat and bleach[cxlvii]

That's what they'll show a tourist[cxlviii]

But New York is a dirty florist[cxlix]

You'll get tangled within its forest [cl]

My roots are sinking in the mud [cli]

While lily petals flourish[clii]

The can, the boot, the cat, the rat[cliii]

Entrenched within the city

The weed, the smog, the haze, the gas,[cliv]

Isn't it all so pretty?[clv]

I'm trying to reach a milli[clvi]

But pigs are just trying to kill me [clvii]

Their bullets tear and pierce my flesh

It all seems to fulfill me[clviii]

A boy with heart who's marked for narc at park[clix]

It's all so shitty

I speak, I flow, my seeds, they grow[clx]

Then POW! I leak, like titty[clxi]

Thank GOD for games and gangs and guns [clxii]

It all makes me so witty

The green is nice and greed's my vice as auto as the city[clxiii]

You see the street is sweet with wheat[clxiv]

Whose task is just to frisk[clxv]

One beat, we meet, I stop my feet

My mouth then goes tisk-tisk

No money to feed the meek and weak [clxvi]

Who squeak because they're poor

We're just some divided states with bait [clxvii]

And plates that feast to war [clxviii]

The city that's gritty, New York City

Has me giddy and fiending for more

Believe that the need to concede in the greed

Is the force behind the gore [clxix]

"Never Liked The Natives"

The poem that follows is one of teaching. It was manifested to provide knowledge and raw ideas for a fast sinking generation. In this day and age, children and teenagers are often so caught up in the latest trends and fashion, that despite the fact that they attend school on a regular basis, they haven't got a clue as to what's going on in the world. Many of them also lack knowledge regarding America's history, especially minorities such as the Blacks and Latinos.

Here, I decided to include a poem that provides a figurative classroom with the essential resources and necessary tools to be enlightened upon what society has failed to teach them. The title, "Substitute" comes from me envisioning myself as a substitute teacher that informs students about historical black figures such as Dr. Martin Luther King Jr., Malcolm X and Huey Newton. I even mention Tupac Shakur and what he potentially could have become in society had he not been gunned down on September 13th, 1996. Ladies and gentleman, what this shows is that the substitute is sometimes better proven in capabilities than the actual instructor. Moreover, it will open the minds of students in a way that the day-to-day teacher simply cannot.

"Substitute"

I am the healer[clxx]

You are my patients[clxxi]

I'm just here to mend you kids[clxxii]

With truth and revelation[clxxiii]

Numbing teeth's a daily duty, nova, cation[clxxiv]

Informing patients every day is truly no vacation[clxxv]

I am from the U.S.A. what does it constitute?[clxxvi]

A stripper's booty on the block, I mean she prostitute[clxxvii]

The teacher is not here today, I am his substitute[clxxviii]

I'm dropping bombs within your ward, I am the parachute[clxxix]

TV is a killer and that's just reality[clxxx]

Children lacking substance, guidance, and morality[clxxxi]

I see star spangled fakes within a parody[clxxxii]

But give them tools to read and write they'll see things validly[clxxxiii]

Forget the space and status bar[clxxxiv]

Just give them clarity[clxxxv]

And give them hope instead of dread tuned into melody [clxxxvi]

Then feed them health instead of junk, I mean a celery[clxxxvii]

I'll quench your thirst for knowledge kids it is a rarity[clxxxviii]

Malik Shabazz, Martin King, Huey Newton, shot[clxxxix]

I guess that means I'm next in line[cxc]

I'm real like...Tupac[cxci]

Translate into modern lingo means I'm just too hot![cxcii]

Shakur these kids with facts and blacks [cxciii]

While you pursue to plot [cxciv]

On how to stop me now because you're scared and I do lots[cxcv]

And kill me way before my time before you cruise your yacht[cxcvi]

And cook the feast not meant for me within your brand new pot[cxcvii]

You never liked the *Native Son* please just won't you stop?[cxcviii]

"A Heinous Reality"

"Real-ity" was a poem I wrote after I got extremely tired of coming across the filth we believe to be "reality" television. I'm sure we've all flicked through the channels and have witnessed some form of reality television in one way or another. Whether it's *Flavor of Love, Basketball Wives, The Real Housewives of Atlanta, I Love New York, The Jersey Shore,* or my favorite one of the entire bunch, *Love & Hip-Hop.* The one thing these shows all have in common is that they all pay a bunch of people, (who I believe will do anything for a quick buck) a modest amount of money to act ignorant and unconstitutional upon the screen.

Over the last few years, the relevance of these shows have been at an all-time high as it seems that every girl and their man has a reality show. I'm not saying that all types of reality shows are bad but many of them exhibit certain creeds and ethnicities as a representation of certain lifestyles that are either exaggerated, fabricated and degrading.

What's worse is that many of these shows including pop culture at large have tremendous influences upon the kids and teenagers of today's generation as they often look to these reality stars for guidance and wisdom.

Therefore, the only thing that I wanted to do with my following poem was to denounce reality television and all that comes with it in ten lines. Also, when performing this poem live, I've noticed that it often takes me fifteen seconds on average to recite it in its entirety as clear as I can. Fifteen seconds which represent the seconds of fame that surround these so-called *"reality"* stars.

"Real-ity"

They can't wait to be rich

They can't wait to be famous

I swear what one does for spotlight is heinous[cxcix]

The season will end, forgetting their name[cc]

All for those fifteen seconds of fame

Love and Hip-Hop's a bitch

She supplies you with drama

While Basketball wives will throw in "yo mama"[cci]

Before you start feeling, hype and vindictive

Remember Reality TV is SCRIPTED![ccii]

"Attention Please"

"LIFE IS REAL!" Seriously, that's all I can say. Often times, life is depicted as something that is vibrant, something that is fruitful, but what it also should be recognized as is something that has many peaks and valleys that are waiting to be fully explored.

While all of this is true, life comes with a bunch of other things that exhibit the daily struggles and fluctuations we deal with as human beings. The way "LIFE IS REAL!" came about is interesting. I remember getting a text message from my good friend Robb who asked me to write a poem that vividly encapsulated the raw ills of life. Upon elaborating more, he said that he wanted it to be as rugged and as hard as I possibly could make it. Additionally, he couldn't have made it any clearer when he said that it should mirror the likes of Nas' *"New York State of Mind"* record off of his 1994 timeless gem, *"Illmatic"*.

The moment he told me this, I eagerly got to work and began thinking of how I would piece it all together. My first attempt was to get it in actual writing as I pulled out a composition notebook and began to write. Although, after a while, I'll admit, it just didn't work for me. After copying all that I had written up until that point into my BlackBerry, the lines suddenly came and within a span of an hour to go along with a few days of vigorous edits, I had written what fully fleshed and formed into my poem now known as "LIFE IS REAL!"

"LIFE IS REAL!"

Your attention please

Your attention I need it

Live from all the masses and the classes just to feed it

So many born to poverty and hunger, yes, I've seen it!

I'll Make It Plain like Malcolm [cciii]

Raw as Eddie and I mean it[cciv]

First, okay, let me tell you what I see

Around these parts of us freedom ain't free[ccv]

As sure as the doctor checks the sample in your pee [ccvi]

Before you take a sip just know it ain't your cup of tea[ccvii]

Kids will never hesitate to say their life has sucked [ccviii]

But truth to the matter is we've gotta up their luck[ccix]

But sit still, we're lame, it is a time to be a duck[ccx]

No guidance or protection and generations fucked [ccxi]

The school system's a trip, I don't like teachers[ccxii]

But not the one within your class they're watching from the bleachers[ccxiii]

They make him think self-image is the most important feature[ccxiv]

He's camping out of ignorance that's why he wants the sneaker[ccxv]

Never stop at nothing to control, they use he![ccxvi]

Bagging for some profit, dimes and nicks, he lose he![ccxvii]

Trying to feed himself within his soul, abuse thee![ccxviii]

Shots unto his face and Newton's dead, Huey! [ccxix]

Enough of this shit man I'm tired of the slander[ccxx]

Time to rebel B, no longer will I banter[ccxxi]

Hooking must stop G, no longer can you man her[ccxxii]

This world is not pink because reality's the camera[ccxxiii]

She said they're used to not having nothing real[ccxxiv]

I want to nourish them man, but only she would feel[ccxxv]

It then went down easy, slipped up, banana peel[ccxxvi]

Digest within her tract like a homeless and his meal[ccxxvii]

LIFE…IS…REAL!

"Life Is No Vacation"

If you're looking for a piece within this book that I consider being a gem, look no further than "Any Means". For one thing, I remember writing it on a train ride back on July 4th 2013. I was headed to a barbeque that my cousin was throwing that day.

Although July 4th is a day that we as Americans observe our independence and the monumental writing of the constitution, there are still things that go on today that show we as a people are far from free. And when I say we, I hope you don't think that I'm specifically speaking for African-Americans or people of color. Instead, I am speaking for people of every race, creed and religion. To some degree I believe we all in some form of capacity are still mentally in shackles.

Until we learn our sole true purpose and reach out amongst one another with peace and love, I believe we as a people have a long way to go until we finally figure out some things on both sides of the coin. These are my reasons for writing "Any Means." Similar to the prior poem, "LIFE IS REAL", it automatically came to me with such authenticity that I knew it to be ideas that had developed within me from becoming socially aware, learning the roots of America's capitalistic and racist society, reading *The Autobiography of Malcolm X* at the age of twenty, *Native Son, and Black Boy* by Richard Wright at twenty-one and from just about anything that aided me in opening my eyes to the real circumstances that minorities endure within the United States of America.

I honestly would like to admit that I even shocked myself when creating the poem because after I completed it, I was surprised on how my skills had vastly improved from over a year's worth of writing, but more importantly, I was surprised as well as proud when I realized how much that I knew in terms of the politics, literature and poor infrastructure of the black community.

"Any Means" (Necessary)

I wrote this on the subway deep in thought, contemplation [ccxxviii]

I thought of all the ills that plague this zone, the nation [ccxxix]

As sure as a Buddhist deep in thought, inflation [ccxxx]

What the fuck is up with us and the rest of the nation? [ccxxxi]

Homeless people lying on the floor? That's crazy [ccxxxii]

When you have the bread for NBA, now pay me [ccxxxiii]

Then you ask for money just to church, so save me [ccxxxiv]

The one percent don't make it to the hoods, they're lazy [ccxxxv]

In life we've come close, but yet, not too far [ccxxxvi]

It's where you'll end up CPR by CPR [ccxxxvii]

Meeting daily quotas for their doors to stay ajar[ccxxxviii]

Courtesy, Professional, Respect, a cop car[ccxxxix]

I think our country doesn't know the truth, fallacy[ccxl]

Plan A will never prosper cause of B, malice see?[ccxli]

Taxing just to kill for oil spills, deserting me[ccxlii]

So fuck the GDP and GOP you're hurting me[ccxliii]

And please, oh please, I want you all to listen

Many things within the books are historically missing[ccxliv]

I think it's time for us to go record *"What Was Written"*[ccxlv]

Complexity of all your souls and minds, the prison[ccxlvi]

But fuck it though, cause you know what? I'm gonna cool out

A new route, bazook out, New Jersey Turnpike shootout[ccxlvii]

I'm talking 'bout Assata, but not Tupac Shakur[ccxlviii]

Panthers like Mutulu are just why I have the floor[ccxlix]

So shout out to every single ghetto boy in the nation[ccl]

And get it by any means because this life is NO VACATION!!![ccli]

Part IV: Generations (A Story)

"Stolen Youth" (I)

"Neighborhood Watch" (II)

"DOWN!" (III)

"Another Black Girl Lost" (IV)

"Black Girl's Son" (V)

Another story consisting of African-American boys, girls, as well as the mothers & fathers within their communities...This is the story of three lost generations...

Okay, so I'm going to give you something different in this section. This is a narrative describing the pain, abandonment as well as the social detriment of many African-American families living within the guttered environment of America's inner cities.

In this section, you will read five interrelated poems built into one overarching story about a woman who gives birth to a child without the father being present. The child then comes of age and makes her own mistakes which then leads to more confusion, bitterness and despair.

In these poems you will come to make your own assumptions and inclinations about what in general is going on and why does it happen to be this way in which you read it.

It's a story that opens up in the late 1970's (1978 to be exact). From there, it progresses into 1994 and comes full circle in 2014. Although this is the second to last section of this book, a majority of these poems were final pieces of writing as I wanted to fully carve out a story that would resonate with readers by creating characters that you've probably come to know within your own daily lives. Thanks to my creative writing background in fiction, it is with my greatest delight that I present to you a lost generation.

"Stolen Youth" (I)

Live from delusion[cclii]

Die in the streets or reside in the ruin[ccliii]

Young souls are lost twisted by all the confusion[ccliv]

So sometimes you can't blame em' cause they don't know what they're doing[cclv]

Trap, crack, lack of maps are really all they've ever had[cclvi]

Raised on the strength of mom cause they never knew their Dad[cclvii]

Slang, gun, gang bang are really all they've ever seen[cclviii]

Breaking news, 5pm, they see their friends on the screen[cclix]

Bap, bap, bap, bap! *"man, what the fuck was that?"*[cclx]

Popping off at the school where my little brother at[cclxi]

Pigs parked on the street, kids rat-tat-tat-tat[cclxii]

Throw the .9 in the sewer, that's just how you hide the gat[cclxiii]

85

And them niggas weak as fuck, yet they try to be the man[cclxiv]

Til' they testify in court and dry snitch on they man [cclxv]

Then their baby have a baby so its catch me if you can[cclxvi]

It's ironic cause the seed will never get to see the man[cclxvii]

Since he placed her on the earth she never seen him since birth[cclxviii]

Young girl seeks attention, she don't really know her worth [cclxix]

And she's dealing with a pimp who just treats her like dirt [cclxx]

So she end up getting hurt by a nigga like Kurt

These are words from the wise, you gotta put God first[cclxxi]

Once you blow all the high, he just helps you at your worst [cclxxii]

Even when you think he'll never have your life reimbursed[cclxxiii]

Say a prayer, keep the faith, no such thing as being cursed[cclxxiv]

Man, these lines come hard, I'm just a dick in the booth[cclxxv]

And I'm jotting down my thoughts just to carve out the truth[cclxxvi]

Like a hungry homeless man with a cup and a tooth [cclxxvii]

Roy's baby was with Ruth[cclxxviii]

Tales of a Stolen Youth[cclxxix]

"Neighborhood Watch" (II)

"I'm built for war, call me an object[cclxxx]

Got bills to pay, have we come to odds yet?[cclxxxi]

That gang wants me, call me a prospect[cclxxxii]

I hate what I see amongst the foul ghetto projects [cclxxxiii]

Roy's on the corner, he's got his pants down[cclxxxiv]

Not comprehending that he's the man now[cclxxxv]

He's gotta step up and feed the fam now [cclxxxvi]

But thanks to that gang member, he's now a man down [cclxxxvii]

Now…Roy's girl is sad, see?[cclxxxviii]

Feeling all alone you can say she's madly

Insane, fuming flames[cclxxxix]

Regrets that their little Asia will never get to know her Daddy[ccxc]

And as for me? Another day, sunshine, I'm in a good mood[ccxci]

Just got word my financial aid was approved [ccxcii]

So I guess that means…I get to further my education[ccxciii]

In other words…I'm in a good mood

But financial aid is starting to bother me[ccxciv]

I had to fight just to get it straight like good barbering[ccxcv]

I'm thinking this while Guy blows pay on lottery[ccxcvi]

Where are dreams that mold from clay? The GOOD pottery[ccxcvii]

You know I now hit the corner store and get sicker [ccxcviii]

Because I see a wino staggering from liquor [ccxcix]

You see he once had a wife but constantly hit her [ccc]

And has now been reduced to nothing while he constantly bickers[ccci]

And so, I guess I'm escaping neighborhood watch as I should

Just one day, who knows, I'll leave this damn place for good [cccii]

And when I'm no longer here, say I did the best that I could [ccciii]

To provide hope and some truth for the youth[ccciv]
.

To make it out of their hoods[cccv]

"Down!" (III)

Listen up, there was a boy at forty-second place

Who had some droopy lips and a swag like Ma$e[cccvi]

That brainless life is what he stake, had to get a taste[cccvii]

But then he disappeared and now he's gone without a trace

Always at the park, may even see him in the mall [cccviii]

Class starts at 8'oclock, he's always in the hall

Went to class one day so teacher quizzed him on the wall[cccix]

He never knew the answer so the boy would always stall[cccx]

The teacher shook her head and so she then said,

"Doll, in my office after class I have to make the call"[cccxi]

Kurt would then reply, *"Bitch, see me in the halls!"*[cccxii]

It hurts me as I write, recite and light this just for y'all[cccxiii]

And no belief in anything so all he did was ball[cccxiv]

And trust me when he did this best believe he gave his all[cccxv]

Then June arrives, 2009, no coats, right? Cool[cccxvi]

Commencement here, another there, he quits High School[cccxvii]

What Kurt did next, he would regret, straight ice cool

He had a gun and craved a whip, a vice, dice, fool[cccxviii]

Someone squealed then came the pigs they said, "Gun down!"[cccxix]

He then dipped behind a truck to squeeze off a round

Was marked on roof, they hit his chest, he then falls down[cccxx]

Lying on the floor in red, he doesn't make a sound [cccxxi]

Captured him and locked him up so now you know he's bound

Sister saying "free my bro" all around the town

He now wears red, I wish it blue, I'm talking cap and gown[cccxxii]

No one's heard from Kurt since, he's probably in the pound[cccxxiii]

"Another Black Girl Lost" (IV)

Okay, remember Asia?[cccxxiv]

Her life is obscene[cccxxv]

She's dealing with some hormones, a boy at 16[cccxxvi]

Joey's in her class and wants to spit at sixteen[cccxxvii]

He's got a baby on the way, she carry his seed[cccxxviii]

Her momma said its Déjà vu, the age of 16[cccxxix]

Where's her proper guidance like a gun and six teens?[cccxxx]

Within a grave or in the jail, her momma never told her[cccxxxi]

All she knows is boys her age, daddy never hold her

And since her Dad was never there she gave it up to Joey[cccxxxii]

So now she got a baby bump, damn she miss the old her [cccxxxiii]

Chilling with her bitches and they fuck for dollars, twerk[cccxxxiv]

Meet her at the corner a negotiation, work[cccxxxv]

Trafficking her body just for pimp to reap the perks[cccxxxvi]

She has to reach a number or he's bound to go biserk [cccxxxvii]

And man she hates that guy you know he really is a jerk [cccxxxviii]

But if she don't cooperate her face will soon be hurt[cccxxxix]

Her face is purple from an Angle handed straight from Kurt[cccxl]

Listen girls, it's never worth it, never be the dirt[cccxli]

Joey left her, she's alone, I guess she was the fool[cccxlii]

To think he'd love her every day she thought she was his jewel[cccxliii]

Forty acres and a mule dazing in a pool[cccxliv]

The baby's here, with no choice, she dropped it out of school[cccxlv]

Here's to Joey cause he got her, guess he was the boss[cccxlvi]

Putting all her trust in him like dental does to floss[cccxlvii]

Or like a coin with heads and tails whenever it is tossed[cccxlviii]

A world with no escape Another Black Girl Lost
[cccxlix]

"THE BLACK GIRL'S SON" (V)

Let's pick up where we last left off, Asia had the baby[cccl]

Now insane and fuming flames, you know she's going crazy[cccli]

He's now a teen and in the house like *"mama you don't faze me"*[ccclii]

Does what he want, her face is gaunt, a ghost like Patrick Swayze[cccliii]

The boy is tough "and shit", he's rough!

The leader of his gang

After fights, they stroll the nights, its four a.m., they hang[cccliv]

A bunch of boys with mom's for Dad[ccclv]

They're nine deep, Wu-Tang[ccclvi]

If Dads were there and if they cared it just makes you say, "dang"[ccclvii]

But back to son, he has his fun, he likes to roll his weed[ccclviii]

His cash is flow, that's where it goes and yet he has a seed[ccclix]

Then Asia gives him money so his laziness proceeds[ccclx]

Now what the fuck is up with that? He's got a kid in need[ccclxi]

The girl says, "Rasheed, he's got your nose, boy, this yo' baby!"

Rasheed then says, "Damn bitch, shut up! It's possible, just maybe."

She asks, *"Nigga, you crazy?"*

He says, *"Ho, don't blame me."*

She asks, *"Ummm what?"*

He says, *"Keep your legs closed baby."*[ccclxii]

So when it's all said and done you know the homie had his fun[ccclxiii]

The girl is lost and cold as frost their baby boy turns one[ccclxiv]

Rasheed, Rasheed, with kid to feed but stays concealed like gun[ccclxv]

Here we go again my friends, a Black Girl's Son...[ccclxvi]

Part V: Family

"Pecan Honey"

To start off my family dedications, it wouldn't be right if I opened this section without focusing on the person who partially helped place me here. The next poem you will read is titled "Aquemini" and it is symbolic of both myself and my late sister, Alexandra's zodiac signs.

When writing this poem, I remember writing it because I truly missed my sister's presence. In fact, to this day, my younger sister and I still talk about her as if she still exists. Alexandra was pretty much like a friend to me as well. I can even go as far to say that she also played a motherly role within my life in a lot of ways.

She taught me a lot about respecting women and how guys should go about talking to girls. As I write this I can recall one time that she was taking me and my little sister Samantha to the movies when I opened the building's door and mindlessly let it slam right in her face. Man, when I tell you she let me have it, boy she let me *have* it that day!

"Boy what the hell is wrong with you? When you see a girl coming towards a door, you hold it for her, end of story," she said angrily.

Look, when I tell you I felt like crap, I felt like *crap*. At the time, I was either ten or eleven-years-old and really didn't understand what she was saying but now as I look back upon that moment, I do. What she did helped transform me into becoming the young man that I am today.

Due to the fact that my parents, being Haitian were never really into the American customs of fashion and appearance, Alexandra would often go out of her way to buy Samantha and I the latest gear in clothing apparel and sneakers. Although I was only a kid at the time, I definitely appreciated all of the things she would do for us. Now that I am a young man, I feel like if there is anyone who owes her so much it's definitely me. I mean, if it wasn't for her, I wouldn't be writing this book of poetry as we speak. I'm sure of it.

I am saying this because when Alexandra was about eight or nine, she told my mom that she wanted a sibling. And so, one day she made my mom accompany her to the grocery store to purchase candy.

When she left the store, she saw my mom talking to the man who later came to be my father. You see, my parents had been together in the seventies before my sister was born but they broke up once my mom decided to leave Haiti in order to travel the world. Therefore, I find it funny that they reconvened outside of a little grocery store in Brooklyn. To me, it only proves that I have a purpose and that I'm supposed to be here.

Now all of this changed in the year 2007. It was the year I turned sixteen. At the time I was a junior in high school, had very good grades, and most of all, I was just being a young, care-free, fun loving teenager. That summer, my parents, little sister and I went on a relaxing vacation to Montreal, Canada but by the time we got back, things quickly began to unravel.

By the end of August, Alexandra would stop by the house often and complain to my mom of some red blots that covered her arms. She complained of itching and how much it was bothering her. After my mom had done her best to help and noticed that it had gotten worse, she then urged her to go to the hospital.

Furthermore, one thing led to another and before we knew it, my sister was in and out of the hospital like clockwork until she finally went into a coma. I remember my Dad going to see her in ICU as often as he could because my mother just couldn't bare it. On one specific visit, the doctors informed him that Alexandra was suffering from a bad case of meningitis. I remember him taking a picture of her on his cell phone and the person I witnessed lying upon the hospital bed was totally unrecognizable and a completely different person. My sister was a heavy set young woman but had ballooned twice her size in a matter of a month. As much as I wanted to visit her, my father refused to let us go because he said that no one under the age of eighteen was allowed in the room.

A few weeks after, I got a taste of life's harsh realities for the first time on Saturday, November 17th, 2007. I remember leaving church that afternoon as Samantha and I had just finished choir rehearsal and were headed home. The church, which is relatively two blocks away from my house wasn't far off as we walked. Upon arrival, my Dad told Samantha and I that he wanted to talk to us. As he sat us in the living room, I wasn't prepared for what he was about to say next.

"Kids, I'm sorry to tell you this, but Alexandra passed away at ten o'clock this morning," he said calmly.

To this day, I remember how everything just felt extremely surreal as he said it. Immediately my world began to plunge into an abyss. Samantha, wasted no time as she immediately began to bawl like a baby on the couch. After a few seconds of digesting the shock myself, I remember that I had joined her.

"Mwe konen ti moun, mwe konen," said my Dad in Haitian Kreyol. His voice cracked as he held us both.

After a moment of consoling us, he went into the kitchen to check on my mother. It was then I remember telling Samantha while in the midst of my tears:

"You know, you hear about or see these things on the news all the time but you never think that it could happen to you," I sobbed in between tears.

My sister thoroughly agreed and nodded her head as she continued to cry.

A few days later after everything had come to pass, my sister was buried at All Saints Church in Great Neck, Long Island. I remember watching her casket being lowered into the pit thinking, "Wow, she's really gone, she's never coming back and I'm never going to see her again."

I remember as people began to leave the gravesite, I walked back to the family car thinking to myself, *"It's up to you now Kev. No more being a little kid. You're going to become something great in this life. You're going to make sure that your family is well taken care of, and that they can all live peacefully and happily. Nothing is going to stop you. You've got to do it and will do it. No more games. It's all up to you because you have to become somebody. You have no choice."*

I truly believe that since that day, I matured far beyond than what I ever could have envisioned for myself. I deeply wanted to become something in life. And not because my parents were pushing and influencing me, but more so because I *needed* to… I *wanted* to…

I realized then that life wasn't a game and I was going to take matters into my own hands and succeed at all costs. I mean, besides being my half-sister, Alexandra (or Sandra as we called her around the house) was my friend, supporter and a powerful motherly figure. If she never lived, neither would I have. Without question, I know I owe her everything that comes my way.

"Aquemini"

Because of her, I am here[ccclxvii]

And for her love, I'll shed a tear[ccclxviii]

My motives and thoughts are sincere[ccclxix]

I know she's in heaven but I wish she was here

Objects are fragile, this thing called life[ccclxx]

And the day that she left me, I struggled through strife[ccclxxi]

I searched for clarity inside of a cabinet when a pain struck[ccclxxii]

Just call it a knife

My heart healed slowly from pain and leisure[ccclxxiii]

Still, I carried on with the procedure[ccclxxiv]

But as I sat within her room

It suddenly struck, no more would I see her

With no other choice I crafted a plan[ccclxxv]

Upon her grave, I decided to fan

I pushed the thoughts and all of my strength

Of a sixteen-year-old becoming a man[ccclxxvi]

The journey may stop but it will never end [ccclxxvii]

I'm truly glad that we had made amends [ccclxxviii]

I thank you Alexandra for being my sister

Until the day, that I see you again

"If I Lose You, I Lose Myself"

This next piece was probably the easiest poem to write. It's about someone in whom if they suddenly weren't here, there would be no reason for me to continue existing. It's about someone who cares about me so much that she's not afraid in telling me that I messed up.

The following piece is dedicated to my younger sister, Samantha Anglade. If anyone on this earth knows me well enough, they would know that Samantha is my best friend. We share tons of laughs, jokes, smiles and we've also cried and experienced many dark moments together.

I really don't know what I would do without her. The day I lose her is the day I lose myself. It's that serious because she is all I have and means that much to me. As kids we really didn't get along which is why I find it funny that we love each other the way we do now.

Nonetheless during our childhood, we were absolutely inseparable. Whether it was school, sleepovers, it was rare for one of us to go somewhere without the other. Even now it's amazing to me in terms of how selfless we are as young adults. For example, we're always willing to share and if one of us borrows money from the other, we never discuss when the other will expect to see that money back. I mean, we trust each other that much.

Growing up, I found my sister to be very annoying, especially when she was going through her pre-teen, pubescent phase. However, all of that was put aside once we lost our sister Alexandra. After our father broke the news to us about her passing, I remember saying to her while in the midst of my tears, "Listen Sam, we can't fight any more, and even if we do, let's promise that we will make up within a twenty-four-hour period okay?"

"Okay," she said through sniffles as I held her close.

And since then, we've gotten into a few disagreements but we have remained true to our word. Now, our relationship is stronger than ever as we never let a situation linger longer than it has to. I remember even as kids when one of us would get candy, snacks, or even a slice of pizza, my mother would always make sure that we shared. Even if we cried she made sure that we knew the reason behind her actions.

"You two are brother and sister, therefore, you're supposed to share," she'd say.

As I think back to that time period and reflect, I'm grateful and thankful for what my mother taught us. Due to her teachings as well as my shared experiences with Samantha, she and I now have an unbreakable bond. We know just how fragile life is and due to the many obstacles that have come our way, we've become the tightest of friends. In my mind there is no doubt that we'll be there for each other until the end of time.

"Twin & Friend"

Where should I start?

Oh I don't know!

So many places

That I can go

Yee-haw!

Let's start the show

On second thought

I'll let it flow

Close because

2 years apart

But your global positioning

Is in my heart

Let's find ourselves

Now that's a start

More welcoming than my own farts

Whatever I gain, is for you

And vice-versa, you support me too

And when I'm down, you see I'm blue[ccclxxix]

You play like Steve, to find the clue[ccclxxx]

Love is crazy and often sought

But when from you, it can't be bought[ccclxxxi]

What's on your mind?[ccclxxxii]

We share some thoughts[ccclxxxiii]

We share because

Our Mom well taught

To love is love

So love thyself

More abundant, than one's own wealth

We must be stable, let's watch our health[ccclxxxiv]

If I lose you, I lose myself[ccclxxxv]

So in a life, where all must sin

And people gulp, Snoop's Juice and Gin[ccclxxxvi]

I'm with you sis, until the end

Let's win! Let's win![ccclxxxvii]

My twin, my friend

"Fallen King"

First off, let me start by saying that this was the last poem I wrote for this section. It's also the third poem I've written for my father and the only one I feel was potent enough to make it into this book. Man, my Dad...Georges Anglade...Where do I start exactly? That's how much of an impact that man has had on my life. He was simply *THAT* incredible! *THAT* awesome!

Now for any of you reading this, before you read the following poem, I would like for you to know that if it wasn't for that man I wouldn't be here. Neither would this book. Unlike many other young black men that I've come across, I have been blessed and fortunate enough to once have had a father within my life.

In addition to that, I was lucky that I didn't have to endure growing up within a broken home, something in which many young urban people of color often identify with.

As much as I'm expressing love for my Dad, I don't want any of you to think he was an easygoing guy. Although he was a very nice man, he was also the strictest adult that I have and will ever come across in my lifetime. Although a militant, no-nonsense, and hard-pressing individual, my father did the things expected of a man when taking care of his family.

My parents moved to Queens with me in 1992 when I was still a baby. Around that time, my father was laid off from a factory job and began to work at Otto Hermann Inc. (a retail store that sold paint, hardware and electrical home appliances) in the Glendale neighborhood of Queens. Every morning my Dad would wake up at 4:30am to go to work. He'd be out the door by five and I wouldn't see him until five in the evening. The reason why I'm writing all of this is to show you what kind of a hard worker my Dad was. In the seventeen to eighteen years he worked at the job, not once did he ever receive a promotion. It's something that truly bothers me because the man worked extremely hard to take care of us and was extremely professional to boot. The fact that they never promoted him for his great work and professionalism is a travesty.

My earliest memories of my father were ones of constant fear. As I've mentioned before, he had a no-nonsense attitude and an aura about him that undeniably commanded respect. Without question, he was most certainly a marvelous man, someone who never hesitated to help when others were in need, someone who would warm up to just about any person he came across. However, make no mistake, if you ever stepped on his toes, especially if you were his kids, he'd, *"kick your ass,"* as I often remember him saying.

Although I never really had a traditional father-son relationship with my Dad, I just can't begin to tell you how influential he was in terms of shaping me into a young man. My father was a Haitian man from the Caribbean and with that being said, he tremendously valued education.

There are so many phrases I can recall him saying to me in a lifetime but some of my favorites are, *"Did you do your homework?" "Where's your report card?" "Use your brain", "I'm not playing games with you Kevin!" "Did you say sorry to your mother?" "What's up young man?"* just to mention a few and he would often say all of these with a thick Haitian accent that he never was able to completely rid himself of even as he lived in America for almost thirty plus years.

As Samantha and I got older, my father loosened the reigns on us a bit. Maybe it was because he noticed that we were maturing, but it wasn't until my late teens that he and I started to talk more and built a relationship. And so, just when I had completed high school and finished my first year of college, that's when I began to lose him…

The summer of 2010, following my freshman year in college was a great one. I had good grades, I had just gotten my driver's license (under the tutelage of my father) and I had a hot Hispanic girlfriend to boot. I remember my Dad looking at me on many occasions and his face showed the same pride each and every time. There was no doubt that he was proud. I think for the first time; he saw his own son becoming a man in every sense of the word.

Nevertheless, as the new school season rolled in and I was set to begin my sophomore year, my Dad started to get extremely sick. I remember there was one Monday morning in September when my Dad didn't feel well and he asked my mother to call an ambulance. After the EMTs and paramedics arrived they checked his blood pressure as well as his vital signs before taking him away.

At the time, I didn't really think much of it, because my father was a very strong man. I had seen him do and conquer so much that I knew he'd bounce back, or so, I thought. A few hours turned into a day, a day had turned into a week and before I knew it, my Dad was in a coma just how Alexandra had been after a seven-day period.

By the time I went to go visit him, the doctors told my mother that he might not make it. This caused great panic within my family as everyone was in and out of the hospital hoping that he'd recover. I even remember visiting on one occasion and recall him looking around the room with IV's attached to his body. My heart was so heavy seeing him in that state and what made it worse was that he briefly had forgotten who he was after getting out of the coma.

A few days later, I can remember visiting him as he seemed to be back to his normal self.

He was speaking and interacting with me as if nothing had ever happened. I was glad that he seemed okay. The doctors had even told him that he would be discharged the following day.

The next day he came home to what felt like a parade. Many family members came over to celebrate his return. There was food, drinks, and everyone was happy. My Dad had chronic Hepatitis B which caused him to develop cirrhosis of the liver. Anyone who knew him knew that he loved to drink alcohol which certainly took a toll on his health. However, as he returned, he vowed to never drink again knowing he had almost lost his life because of it.

On Sunday, October 10th, my father celebrated his 59th birthday. After wishing him a happy birthday and giving him a gift, (a glass monument) he thanked me for the well wishes and said that if it hadn't been for God, he wouldn't have been alive. The irony of that moment was that nine days after commemorating his day of birth, he was called home by the heavenly father. I remember that 19th day of October as if it were yesterday. I was in English class when my cellphone started to vibrate from within my pocket. When I had gotten the chance to step out and look at the caller I.D., I saw that I had been left a voicemail to go along with a missed call. I then stepped out of class and quickly dialed my voicemail when I heard his voice,

"Hi, Kevoo[ccclxxxviii], it's Daddy, I went back to the hospital. Come visit me when you get out of school," he said.

Are you serious? I thought as I went back into class.

Later that day, I nervously fumbled with the car door of my Dad's Chrysler as I opened it and ignited the ignition. After getting onto the highway, I speedily made my way to Jamaica Hospital. Upon arrival, I was informed that he was in a holding room. By the time I had found it, a doctor had pulled back some curtains and there he was, lying on a stationary bed.

"How are you feeling?" I asked.

"Not too good," he replied in a weak voice.

"I tried calling you once I left school but I couldn't reach you. Where's your phone?"

"At home," he said.

"Why don't you have it?"

"I don't need it anymore," he replied.

"What do you mean?" I asked nervously.

It was the first time after frequent visits that I ever recalled being truly scared.

"Look," he said, "Go home, okay? Go home, and make sure you do all of your homework."

I laughed a little, internally, when he had said that. Even within a very tense situation that teetered in between the matter of life and death, here he was worrying about homework.

"Alright, well mommy is coming to see you soon," I responded.

"Okay," he replied as he gave me his wallet and driver's license.

After examining them carefully, I noticed specs of shiny red blots. It seemed as if he had been coughing up blood prior to my arrival.

Little did I know that same Tuesday evening, that I would never have another conversation with him again as he passed away later that night. My mother had gone to see him at the hospital when my sister came into my room a bit after midnight and started wailing.

"Kevin, Daddy died!" she screeched in the midst of frantic tears.

I immediately wasted no time as I began to cry hysterically.

"NO!" I bellowed continuously until the word grew tired of pouring out of my mouth.

It just couldn't be. Not the man who constantly reprimanded me if I did anything wrong. Not the man who taught me the value of education. Not the man who worked his ass off, daily, in order to support his family. It couldn't have been real. At the time, I thought it was just a dream.

Over the next week and a half, everyone and anyone who meant something to me or my father would offer their words of encouragement.

"Stay strong," I heard. *"Everything will be okay." "You're the man of the house now."*

I remember the night of my father's wake, my uncle Joseph through marriage on my mother's side told me to write down his eulogy as I was scheduled to give it the following morning at his funeral service.

"Whatever you are going to say, make sure that you write it down tonight," he said.

"But how could I possibly write anything down?" I thought.

The man had been an inspiration not only to me, but to a plethora of others as well.

"No," I said to myself.

Anything said about my Dad will be done the right way. All from the heart... I thought.

The day of his service, I don't know what got into me, but the only thing I do know was that it wasn't me. God had penetrated my body and blessed me with the words to give my father a great farewell. I stood at the pulpit as I provided the speech but by the time I was done I received a standing ovation. I saw that my words had resonated with everyone who ever knew him and in that moment, although I didn't show it, I was proud to be an Anglade, as well as proud to be his son.

Not too long after, I came to the conclusion that there was a reason for my father summoning me to the hospital that day. It was almost as if he was passing down the torch from one generation to the next. He was certain of what I was capable of and knew that his family would be in the best of hands. He didn't have to say it with words but the fact that I was the last family member to see him alive says everything.

My father had been a man of purpose and that encounter was definitely planned. I'm certain that Georges Anglade is one of, if not, the strongest man that I will ever come across in my lifetime. In his passing, I came to realize that my father had been more than just a father, he was my hero. In other words, he saved me from me before I even got a chance to indulge within the crime riddled environment in which I grew up in and for that I am truly thankful.

"Legend"

I remember the day of your passing, I promised I wouldn't cry

Until I heard R.A. the Rugged Man's *"Legend's Never Die"*[ccclxxxix]

And no, they never die

Instead they all just fly[cccxc]

And then some seeds behind their souls will grow and multiply[cccxci]

Hey Dad, I really miss you man like Vietnam vet and son[cccxcii]

Or like a putrid ugly cop who's searching for his gun[cccxciii]

And man? I fear none

I'm bright, just like the sun

Who would've thought the weight I'd come to lift would scale in at a ton[cccxciv]

Three years you've been gone

So know I am the man

You left us prematurely, now I do the best I can

I just received my Bachelors, I'm crafting a Master plan[cccxcv]

I think that you'd be proud to know I'll go for Masters man

I've inherited all of your jewelry so money just ain't a thing[cccxcvi]

You're everywhere I dare to go, I'm always wearing your ring[cccxcvii]

And yes it does bling, my heart for you sings

Flying high to be the best, your parenting gave me wings[cccxcviii]

Oh Dad, I do miss you, and oh how I really would like to kiss you[cccxcix]

Right now there's many issues man that's fucking up my mental

You were hard, but me? I'm gentle

I'm fragile like led pencil

You chewed me up like dental

I've learned your time on earth was rental[cd]

It all makes sense now

I've traced you like a stencil[cdi]

All the things that we went through

It was all just really meant to

124

Make me stronger, taller, brighter, your message was even tighter

Never on the streets but believe that I am a fighter[cdii]

Kristina? No longer with her, she drowned me Dad like liquor[cdiii]

You liked that I was with her but I just had to dismiss her

Her love was cold like winter and real fresh like new elixir[cdiv]

She never showed to say goodbye[cdv]

For your namesake I ditched her

Thanks for staying on my ass cause life is no vacation[cdvi]

Banned TV every damn school day, I'm talking 'bout PlayStation[cdvii]

I saw it on the weekends then Sundays I gave it back

Dad I have no time for games

It could have been my crack[cdviii]

Thanks pop for class and suits and smarts, they're all good ties[cdix]

Your drive, the strive, they're all alive [cdx]

A Legend Never Dies.

"Grandma's Boy"

One of the last few pieces within this book of poetry belongs to my late maternal grandmother, Yvette Bellvue. I swear, if there was any other person in whom I can truly say that I would trust my life with other than my sister Samantha it would have to be my grandma.

A no-nonsense woman from Jacmel, a township of Haiti, my grandmother was the definition of a strong black woman. Although I don't know a lot about her past, I do know that she had a rough childhood. One in which her mother (who was white) passed away before my grandmother could even talk, and as far as her father was concerned, she really didn't talk about him much. All I know for sure is that she grew up in a foster home and eventually became an independent woman who worked, owned a house, and single handedly, raised six children.

The reason why I loved my grandmother so much was because I spent the most time with her in my early days compared to everyone else. She would bathe me as a child, feed me, tell stories and would sometimes sit with me and watch some of my favorite television programs. Simply put, she was my protector. As a kid growing up, my sister Alexandra had her own room, while my parents obviously had their own. Therefore, my grandmother and I slept in the same bed. As a kid, I thought that as long as she was around, I wouldn't have anything to fear.

It wasn't until a few years later that I realized there was a thing out there called death. It came whenever it wanted and it promised that everyone is susceptible to it at one point in time or another. The thought of it scared me and I remember many nights getting on my knees and praying to God that his son Jesus Christ would eventually come down upon earth as part of the resurrection. Therefore, once he did, my grandmother wouldn't have had to face death. I also remember asking God in helping me to invent a time portal. That way if I sensed that my Grandma was in danger of losing her life, I could rewind time so that she'd be alive and well.

As I think about it now, I can't believe what a silly kid I was. And it's because of those thoughts I had as a kid that I find it amazing in how they perceive the world. Children are often so honest that their innocence blinds them from the harsh and cruel realities that we must all come to terms with. The reality being that for everyone who comes and steps foot upon concrete, they must perish in due time. No one lives forever, however, what we do with the allotted time we possess is what matters more than anything.

With that being said, I remember exactly when my grandmother started to fade away. It was December of 2009 and by that time, she had long moved out of my family home and was living with my aunt in Easton, Pennsylvania. It was Christmas weekend and my mom wanted us all to go see her as a family. I can't really express how I felt, but I knew that what came out of the kitchen couldn't have been my grandma. Her appearance was of one that had lived through many wars and battles throughout the majority of their life. She also looked older in comparison to the last time I had seen her and visibly weak as well.

As I observed her carefully, it was the first time that I noticed her trudging along the dining room with an unfamiliar walker. The looks on our faces from my father, mother, and sister were ones of complete shock. We had heard that she wasn't in the best of conditions however, none of us expected that it would be that bad. It turned out that my grandmother had developed three types of cancers. Stomach cancer, bladder cancer and another one that I'm not too sure of. At the time I was really sad because the person who had taken care of me all throughout my childhood was gone and I knew she would never be the same.

In the year and a half that followed the initial shocker, I was heavily annoyed and angry whenever my mother said we were scheduled to visit her.

"Why do we have to go?" I would say.

"Don't ask questions, we're going," she would respond forcefully.

It wasn't until after my grandmother passed that I realized why I never liked going. Subconsciously, I didn't want to admit that my best friend was suffering right before my eyes and I wanted to either go back in time or remember her just the way I wanted to. A loving being who was happy, loved to smile, and always willing to tend to her grandchildren.

A few months later in May of 2011, my grandmother passed, but during the time of her death I had been prepared for it. It was then that I knew I was no longer a child as I had long put my selfish desires away and was glad to know that my grandmother had been given peace. Besides all of the great advice that she shared with me throughout the years, I learned from my aunt Ghislaine the day of her funeral that the last thing she said in regards to me was "finish school".

As I sat in the limousine while on the way to my grandmother's burial, I thought to myself, *"that's definitely something grandma would say."* Furthermore, as sure as I had made promises to myself upon my sister, Alexandra's grave, as sure as I had been passed the torch from one generation to the next after the death of my father, I then had yet another thing to accomplish and I wouldn't for the world let her down.

"Immortal"

Every time that I prayed at night I prayed for you best friend.

For God would listen, grant my wish

Your life would never end[cdxi]

Maybe I'd invent an elixir and you would then become immortal[cdxii]

I never worked on rewinding time, I was supposed to make a portal[cdxiii]

All these thoughts came in and out, one's imagination ran wild[cdxiv]

It's safe to say that along with a few others,

 I was attached as your grandchild[cdxv]

So in a world as quick as this where days are sure in seven

No woman will ever surpass Yvette[cdxvi]

The Bellvue suites in heaven[cdxvii]

"SuperWoman"

Within this section of poetry, the poems that came before this shape up the final piece that I present to you. This final piece, although brief, entails what exactly my mother has been dealing with since 2007. Throughout this entire section you've come across the burdens and heartaches that I've been challenged with in generally a short amount of time, but the person I applaud in terms of getting through these countless ordeals constantly is my mother. Without her, I really don't know where my sister, Samantha and I would be.

My mother, Jocelyne Marie Joseph, has always been a kind and thoughtful person. In fact, everyone who I have come across in my short existence thus far, appreciates and loves her as an individual. Sometimes people wonder what she's thinking internally because she rarely spoke her mind unless there was something of grand importance to say.

I remember not long after the passing of my sister Alexandra, my mom had become severely depressed. I honest to God didn't think much about how the situation affected her but it wasn't until I spoke to my grandmother about it, that I finally began to understand the issues my mother was dealing with. I remember sitting down with my grandmother one time in the kitchen and she said,

"Kevin, let me tell you something. A mother should never have to bury her own child. Just imagine, you take care of the child, you feed her, clothe her, take her to school, and discipline her. Do you know how hard it is to lose that? Especially the very first one?"

After hearing what my grandmother had to say on the matter, I couldn't help but understand what she was getting at. After all, she had lost one of her very own daughter's named Jeanette just when I was born.

Listening to my grandmother speak upon the dilemma, although I couldn't personally relate, I nonetheless did my best to empathize and feel what my mother felt from a parental perspective. A parent is supposed to have a child bury them, not the other way around. And from that point forward, I watched my mother become a bitter individual right before my very own eyes. Often more times than not, I thought she would never be cheerful again.

I remember the year following my sister's death, my mother was still a little depressed but I thought that she was finally overcoming the loss. I can recall my younger sister and I saying,

"Hey mom, Thanksgiving is coming, what are we doing this year?"

The answer we received was definitely one that we hadn't been expecting, as our mom looked at us with a blank stare on her face and replied,

"From now on, I don't care about Thanksgiving. I don't care about Christmas. I don't care about anything!"

Even my Dad who was lingering around when we had asked her the question remained silent. At the time, we all tried to stay positive, but just when we thought we had conquered one hurdle, was when we were once again, always facing another.

My father's demise was the one that really set my mother over the top. In an instant, she went from being the second source of income (behind my father) to the sole bread winner.

At times, my mother wasn't sure how she would deal with all of the bills as well as the mortgage that was due every month. And it was at that point in time, my mom had desperately wanted me to get a job but I constantly duck and dodged her. Although I was sure that she was struggling, I knew that getting a job would mess up my studies at school. I knew that I wouldn't have thrived if I would have attempted to balance the two. It wasn't until later that my mom came to realize I was so busy trying to figure out my own way, that I knew once I began to prosper and excel within whatever it was that I had a passion for, I would become a stable force that would aid in supporting the family.

My mother has watched me build myself up day-by-day and brick by brick as a writer and also as a small business owner as I've started a small indie press from scratch called Flowered Concrete. Moving forward, I hope to be the most successful indie book publisher in the industry (especially being a black man) as well as one of the top-ranked industry execs in the world. My thoughts are that this journey will be a successful one. I owe it to my father, I owe it to my sister, I owe it to my grandmother but most importantly, I owe it to my mom and I solemnly swear that I won't let her down.

"Observations"

I saw the ache within your eyes

the day you lost your daughter[cdxviii]

You couldn't take the chronic pain

the way that she had suffered[cdxix]

Life is built on tragedies

for some, it's even rougher[cdxx]

By God's grace, upon every day

I saw you had gotten tougher[cdxxi]

No one else that I personally know can take it as you did

You persevered and carried on

Liable for two kids[cdxxii]

So put your hands up in the air

I'll scream for you aloud

Your only son will always say:

"Hey mom, you've made me proud"[cdxxiii]

About The Author

Kevin Anglade is an emerging writer, hip-hop poet, actor, and educator from Queens, New York. He published his first book, *Tales of the 23rd Precinct* (a short-story collection) through his indie press, Flowered Concrete in January of 2013. Moreover, Anglade was featured on NBC's final season of *The Debrief with David Ushery* in 2014 where he provided insight and purpose about his press as a small publisher in NYC. Prior to poetry, the artist got his start through acting, which he believes was the opening of realms that has led him into other artistic dimensions. Now 25, Anglade holds an A.S. in Theatre, (Queensborough Community College) a B.A. in English (Brooklyn College) and is currently pursuing his M.A. in English (Queens College). When he isn't writing or performing, the author enjoys music, a good ol' stand-up comedy routine and just about anything that keeps his heart light and void of harmful energy. *Life Comes From Concrete* is his first poetry memoir.

About The Contributor

Dautchley Desmarais was born on August 6th, 1994 in Mirebalais, Haiti. At the age of three, he and his family immigrated to the United States and found solace in Brooklyn, New York. Inspired by hip-hop and his favorite artist, Tupac Shakur, Desmarais decided to take poetry seriously. After graduating from Gotham Professional Arts Academy, he continued to study the arts and is enamored with its many vocations. By taking part in many open mics and performing on the subway trains, Desmarais sees the impact that his words have on people and wants to stay committed to being his true self. His forthcoming debut collection of poems is titled, *The Flower After The Storm.*

Also By Kevin Anglade

"Life Comes From Concrete": A Poetry Memoir (1st edition)

www.kevinanglade.com

Twitter & Instagram: @velevek

www.kevinanglade.wordpress.com

LOWERED CONCRETE

ⁱ I often remember dreaming every night as a kid.

ⁱⁱ As I've gotten older, I've found it much harder to remember my dreams. Maybe that's just a part of growing up.

ⁱⁱⁱ I'm saying here that hopefully I haven't dreamed as much because I'm slowly beginning to live out everything I've always wanted to be.

^{iv} A very sparse line of nouns but it packs a punch. Firstly, I'm relating the borough of Brooklyn and "Notorious" together as an ode to deceased hip-hop legend Notorious B.I.G. and secondly, I bring in "criminals" to tie everything together as Brooklyn was a very dangerous place during the nineties.

^v Here, I'm saying that the innocence a six-year-old possesses is one that relates in more so of a Godly sense. At that age, you haven't experienced life to the point where you've been condemned or scrutinized by society and also you don't have to worry about education, a career, and the real world as of yet.

^{vi} In 1997, my older sister, Alexandra, was playing with a lighter and accidently set her bedroom on fire. After alerting my parents who were in their bedroom watching television, they (with the help of my maternal grandmother) quickly proceeded into action and manually put out the flames themselves with cups and buckets we had lying around the house (Close call). Also, heaven is mentioned here in irony compared to how it was used in the previous line.

^{vii} In August of 2007, I was in Georgia for the summer at a local community pool when I went into the deep end chasing after some friends and almost drowned. It was a nearby swimmer who jumped in and saved me. I couldn't swim. Thank God...

^{viii} After my older sister, Alexandra, died, I vowed to become something in life. I wasn't exactly sure what but I knew even then that I wanted to do great things and have an impact that resonated in my family. I no longer considered myself an

everyday ordinary sixteen-year-old teenager but as a sixteen-year-old young man.

[ix] After my father passed, I remember thinking to myself that life was just wrong. I couldn't grasp the reality or come to terms on how everything had happened so fast. I once again had to cope with losing a family member. But this time a parent...

[x] The day that my father died at Jamaica Hospital was the day that I became the man of the house. I was conflicted and internally shattered because my protector, my shield, the man who kept me from harm and provided a path for me was no longer around to help me navigate this world.

[xi] April 24th, 2011, Easter Sunday.

[xii] I was headed home (driving) with my sister Sammie in our father's Toyota Landcruiser.

[xiii] When a white van crashed into it. From there, the truck proceeded to spin out of control. Luckily for us, there had been no oncoming cars from behind or up ahead and if there were, it would have caused a massive pile up. I swear God is so amazing! Shouldn't I have been dead already? Another close escape...

[xiv] On January 24th, 2013, I was diagnosed by my primary care physician with Hepatitis B. I contracted the virus by sharing razors with my father when he was alive. I hadn't known about it until then. Once I found out that I was suffering from a chronic case of the condition, I initially thought that I wouldn't make it to see the end of the year.

[xv] My mother and sister stuck by me through the adjustment period and assured me that they would help me get through it.

[xvi] It's a blessing that I'm still here. Although I suffer from the condition there is no doubt that I could have been worse off. All in all, it is better to be alive than dead.

[xvii] Never take life for granted. Live it honorably and respectfully.

[xviii] Stay away from negativity and be positive. You're only as good as you think you are.

[xix] A reference to the 1990's established Nick Jr. children's show, *Blue's Clues* that ran on throughout the decade.

[xx] Be yourself and fight to achieve your dreams. Sometimes it is best to keep them to yourself because critics will try and deter.

[xxi] We're all human beings and thus with that being said, we live, we learn, and experience our daily lives upon the concrete we all walk upon.

[xxii] When young, people often have plenty of nicknames that their friends call them by. As I got older, I wanted to be recognized for just who I was and denounced all nicknames except for stage name(s) that I found to be suitable. (Kev Elev)

[xxiii] I'm Kev, short (a clipping) for "Kevin" and I have a kind heart that wants to help change the world. Thus, where the word "plea" comes in.

[xxiv] During my time as an undergrad in college, I maintained a 3.5 grade point average while juggling skills as an actor, writer, poet, and journalist. I allude to the popular nine-man hip-hop collective (considered by many hip-hop purists to be the greatest hip-hop group of all-time) the Wu-Tang Clan to show how versatile, eccentric and complex my mind and skills are.

[xxv] In this line I'm deliberately and sarcastically poking fun at the United States government as they went to war against Iraq in 2002. The war lasted for ten years and finally came to a "supposed" end in 2012. The line serves as a homophone with I 'rack' street lingo for a thousand dollars. The word "city" is also mentioned two lines prior to this one and alludes to the 2012 stripper hit anthem "Rack City" by Los Angeles rapper Tyga. What I'm ultimately saying here is that our communities as well as our poor class citizens are struggling to get by due to lack of finances, but somehow, we have large sums of money for war and other foolish things.

[xxvi] 'Jerry' is my middle name and I only come out for "cheddar", a slang word for cheese which is street talk for money.

[xxvii] *Tom and Jerry* is an old and popular cartoon that played on Cartoon Network. It has gone on to be one of the most famous well-known trademarks of the Hannah Barbara entertainment corporation.

[xxviii] Hence, I use "Jerry" the mouse, and also the protagonist of the series to give myself a shout out.

[xxix] Here, I'm saying that I have a list full of dreams that I have yet to accomplish. And to make this comparison one that is stark and vivid, I reference Coolio, a Compton-based gangsta rapper from the G-funk era, best known for rapping the kid friendly show tune for Nickelodeon sitcom, *Kenan & Kel* during the 1990's. Also, Coolio, in actuality had dreads, therefore, my list of goals are as long as his dreads once were.

[xxx] On August 24th, 2012 a thirteen-year-old Brooklyn boy by the name of Ronald Wallace was gunned down in Brownsville, one block away from his home. It was approximately 12:45am when the boy was hanging out with friends when the heinous act occurred. I also reference cirrhosis, (the scarring of the liver) in which, if not monitored, can and eventually, will kill due to liver failure. The reason why I bring it up is to metaphorically allude to the death and decay happening everyday within our streets as well as the scarring of a family after losing their loved one. Additionally, this is a slight reference to my Dad as he died from cirrhosis, to go along with his Hepatitis B as well.

[xxxi] We often hear the phrase that "life is a bitch" This line here metaphorically symbolizes that life is fickle. You can be here today and gone tomorrow. Therefore, it isn't meant to be trusted. In addition, *Life's a Bitch* was the third single off of Queensbridge native and hip-hop legend Nas' critically-acclaimed debut LP *Illmatic*, which is often considered as a magnum opus record for the genre by the culture itself. Released on April 19th, 1994, the album is deemed as a lyrical

masterpiece which galvanized the rugged hardcore east coast hip-hop sound in the 90's.

[xxxii] Leaders of the New School was a short-lived Long Island, New York based hip-hop group that featured a young Busta Rhymes. Here, I'm saying that, like a young Busta, I lead a generation of the next up –and-coming poets and emcee's.

[xxxiii] I'm nice at putting words together. I'm clever with my pen.

[xxxiv] Here, I am saying that these lines I put together are more than just rhymes, lines and words. Sticking to the mission statement of my indie press, Flowered Concrete, I am trying to teach you something; Also, I'm giving it to you straight, raw and harsh. All while being as clever and as masterful with the words like Nas' *Illmatic* which ties in the latter portion of the poem together.

[xxxv] My words are effortless, they flow just as if they were an oncoming river bank; a simile.

[xxxvi] As every word flows out of my mouth, they hit you just like a river drops into the course of a stream; A waterfall; Also, I end the line with the word "poem" as if in this scenario, it's a homophone that sounds as if I'm actually pouring the words out of my mouth like a river; Poem = po'em=>pour them

[xxxvii] 16 bits equates to sixteen lines in this poem. Also, SEGA, a popular game console in the 1990's operated on a sixteen-bit processor for their video games. It was certainly, without question, the most popular system of that decade; and as for the second half of this poem, I was twenty-one when I wrote it. Literally two years removed from the age of nineteen.

[xxxviii] Conceived and born in Kings County, better known as the borough called "Brooklyn" but raised in Queens, also known as the sister county to Kings.

[xxxix] I sometimes feel as if Queens is the forgotten borough within New York City, (next to Staten Island) which makes me rep it even harder.

[xl] Life, in actuality, is not a game but I go with it as it comes.

[xli] Back in the day, music lovers usually had tape decks where they would listen to their music as they went about their day. Here though, I am saying that my deck, (which is my tablet) is what I use to go about my day as I listen to music.

[xlii] Every day I try to be the best young role model that I possibly can be. As a young black man and as a man in general.

[xliii] Life is simple. You either make good or bad choices.

[xliv] Now that my Dad is gone, his brother, my uncle/godfather is the next best thing I have in terms of having a father.

[xlv] Ever since my Dad passed, I've stepped up and have tried to be a man to the best of my capabilities.

[xlvi] My sister, my best friend, Samantha Anglade. Also an allusion to the 1990's teen/family sitcom *Sister, Sister* which starred child celebrity twins, Tia and Tamera Mowry. The show aired on ABC from 1994-95 and The WB later on from 1995-1999.

[xlvii] Without my sister, my existence would be pointless and as harsh and painful as a blister.

[xlviii] I'm doing my best to set an example for the generation that comes after me.

[xlix] I'm constantly going through changes and so is the entire community. Also, current events are assignments you get in junior high school that speaks upon everyday social and critical issues.

[l] I'm never late because I'm always on time to relay a good message and spread a good word.

[li] Destiny is not a girl but in fact a metaphor for my actual pursuit in achieving my dreams and what I hope to accomplish one day.

[lii] Aleve is a pain-killing tablet used to treat headaches and reduce fevers. I reference it here to show that Destiny is always sedating my tensions and anxious fears. Therefore, if Destiny was a girl in a physical sense, she'd be calming my

stress in a taxi cab like Aleve would do for someone within their medicine cabinet.

[liii] Destiny will sue my dreams if I'm apprehensive about them.

[liv] Destiny has promised to hold me like Elmer would do to glue it; Google: *Elmer's Glue.*

[lv] If I take my time and focus on myself, Destiny and I will eventually cross paths.

[lvi] As long as I work hard, my work ethic will lead me to my Destiny.

[lvii] As sure as a thief would perform a home invasion or a cop hands you a summons, I'm actually not that far from my Destiny. It is surely coming in due time...

[lviii] In comparison to a Jordan product, it won't cease and stop the massive interest in it because we all need to reach our Destiny in order to survive.

[lix] I need Destiny as bad as those criminals in the 1995 critically-acclaimed drama heist feature-length *Heat*, which starred Robert DeNiro and Al Pacino.

[lx] I need my Destiny just as bad as the U.S. government wanted Osama Bin Laden. This entire line is a clever wordplay on his name.

[lxi] Once I reach my Destiny, my mother will be well off and taken care of. All her financial struggles will finally cease.

[lxii] It turns out that my destiny wasn't a girl after all, but just me writing this silly and ambitious poem within my head. I'll achieve everything that I plan on accomplishing though...in due time...

[lxiii] I am currently twenty-three years of age as I write this and there is so much that I would like to achieve. However, life is flimsy, and as you've probably noticed, this first section of the book deals with uncertainty, doubt, and longevity. Man, I just want to make it to thirty-years-old. That's all I'm asking God for.

[lxiv] It's crazy how life isn't guaranteed and that tomorrow is promised to no one.

[lxv] Everything was in place and stable until I received the news that a girl that I had been in love with had passed away.

[lxvi] Since life has turned its back on me, I'm thinking upon how I may possibly be next in the grand scheme of things.

[lxvii] As human beings, while it is good to plan for tomorrow, it is always best if we take things day by day.

[lxviii] The night of my father's passing, the word was that he had collapsed inside of my house but somehow managed to dial my neighbors for help. Also, my Dad was about 6'1" or 6'2" in height, therefore, it was the last time that he was vertically tall in a physical sense.

[lxix] If I knew what was soon to come and had psychic powers, I would have called Bianca and warned her of the impending danger to come. If it had been left up to me, there would have been no way that she would have left the safe comfort of her home.

[lxx] The world we live in is comparable to a lottery system. We're all trying to prosper as well as elevate to achieve something that we've never thought imaginable.

[lxxi] When playing basketball, it is natural for a pure shooter to habitually count the seams of the basketball in hand especially when shooting from long range. Here, I am articulating that we, as people, are all hoping to live long enough to see success and as we take risks to reach our goals as well as our deepest desires, we're following through by putting the work behind it to make it happen.

[lxxii] The moment that you enter this world, you are destined to die. End of story.

[lxxiii] Another basketball reference that ties the few lines above it all together.

[lxxiv] I'm living smart by not doing the things that would certainly lead me to an early path towards the grave. After experiencing personal loss and suffering through grief, it fueled me to make something out of myself and to strive for my goals.

[lxxv] If I ever die violent, it will be due to excessive force like the way Fred Hampton died; Fred Hampton was an African-

American activist and deputy chairman of the Illinois chapter of the Black Panther Party. He was murdered while sleeping in his apartment. Here, I am ultimately saying that if I, by any chance, am assassinated, it will be because of the radical and aggressive tone of my poems.

[lxxvi] My lyrics and words hold weight due to their valid truths. With them, I see everything that is going on all around me. And it is because of me and how I present myself that will cause America to fear me in this day and age.

[lxxvii] My fellow black brothers praise and respect my lyrics due to their radical tones and revolutionary remarks. Also, these lyrics cause an uproar on the opposing side. My lyrics have so much potential, that those alphabet boys also known as the FBI (Federal Bureau of Investigation) obliquely observe my lyrics from afar as they conspire to take me out.

[lxxviii] I'm hesitant with how much power the words have and after witnessing its effects, I start to think that maybe it would be better if I just happen to keep my thoughts to myself but too late, the FBI can't seem to take it anymore and decide to put a plan into action.

[lxxix] One night, as I'm sleeping, the FBI or local authorities may finally head over to my home and assassinate me; This is an allusion once again to Fred Hampton's death as he was murdered in his apartment on December 4th, 1969, after being shot in the head from point bank range during his sleep. Also, the lines that come before foreshadow this outcome. In addition, three quarters of this poem is autobiographical while the remaining quarter depicts my stance on the use for poetry as a means of resistance and plays out as a "what-if" scenario that alludes to the death of the martyr, Fred Hampton.

[lxxx] In my sophomore year of college during winter break, I wrote a deeply heart-felt crushing letter to my estranged girlfriend one night. I knew that she would never read it, but I had to get it off of my chest, regardless if it ended up in her

hands or not. After writing it, I cried because I couldn't understand why she neglected me.

[lxxxi] Throughout my contemplation of wondering whether this girl had broken up with me, I often felt as if I wanted to die. As tough as I pretended to be on the exterior, it honestly was killing me inside.

[lxxxii] I was really depressed at this time, due to the passing of my father and the neglect that I received from this girl; The word "gloomy" is symbolic in terms of how I felt and the kind of day it was "climate wise" when I met her. It also foreshadows our fate as a couple.

[lxxxiii] We often associate beauty with flawless, however, sometimes the most beautiful things are rotten to their core.

[lxxxiv] I was so head over heels for this girl, that I lost myself during the process.

[lxxxv] Due to the fact that I always wanted to be with her, it kind of altered my relationship with my sister, Samantha.

[lxxxvi] Since her abrupt departure, my sister and I are the best of friends again.

[lxxxvii] She left me and wasn't coming back; Nair is a human hair product preferably for woman, which allows them to remove hair from their body. In essence, it is a light shaver that glides over a woman's skin.

[lxxxviii] This girl is certainly a part of my past now. I'd be wasting time if I continue to talk about her. Also, this plays with the word "sound" as she is no longer relevant, therefore, I don't speak about her.

[lxxxix] I've found myself as if I caught my soul before it was too late. I compare this to a rebound, a play in basketball where players beneath the rim secure the ball in order to give their team either an offensive or defensive possession.

[xc] It took me a while to realize that she was only using me for the moment to feel better about herself as she, too, was

attempting to recover from a heartbreaking relationship prior to being in one with me. Ironic isn't it?

[xci] Here, I use a baseball reference. Metaphorically, I'm saying that if a team's pitcher leaves the mound without prior notification of doing so, then he, as a player, has bailed out on his team, which is exactly what this girl's boyfriend did to her prior to her meeting me.

[xcii] There would be times when I noticed she would text him. Matter of fact, she always texted him under a nickname called "Teddy". Me, being naïve, I should have known that that was an alarming sign of the times to come...

[xciii] I had taken Kristina to her prom when I myself was nineteen, just one year removed from high school. The day of her prom she reconnected with her ex-boyfriend and they conversed as if I wasn't present. That made me furious and livid to the point where I had to venture somewhere for a moment and cool off in order to regain my composure.

[xciv] Slightly referencing the old Christmas saying, *"Twas the night before Christmas"*. Also, I'm saying that it was beautiful and went by extremely fast.

[xcv] Our relationship took off approximately one month of getting to know each other. In all retrospect, looking back at such a time, I can now see that we didn't know each other too well at all. Also, "love" is italicized and put into quotations because now I laugh at the idea that I thought it was real *love*.

[xcvi] At this point in time, I'm currently dating a new girl who I am giving my time in my attempt to get to know her better. It took me about two and a half years to recover from the wound that Kristina left and in some ways, I'm still smarting from it. However, I can't use my past as a reason to hold the next person accountable...No one should...

[xcvii] Same thing, different day = Love

[xcviii] My new girl's love for me helps ease the pain of my last relationship. Also, I use the term fade-away, which is another basketball reference in this poem which adds to a few others

scattered throughout this book; Basketball is my favorite sport, hence, all of the references involving the sport.

[xcix] My current girlfriend has promised to be with me forever. Also, a one-way route is usually a narrow or tiny street where motor vehicles exclusively operate in one direction due to its lack of accommodating space.

[c] On Tuesday, summer nights, I always pass by Kristina's house while on my way to a men's prayer service and on the way back. I've never seen her or her family members come out whenever I've walked that path, however, I always observe the home as it brings back vivid memories of her.

[ci] Bethel Gospel Tabernacle, the church in which I attend these weekly Men's meetings and which I go to for Sunday service.

[cii] If it wasn't for the weekly Tuesday men's meetings at Bethel, I wouldn't be as positive and as spiritual as I am now. Bethel Gospel Tabernacle is a place in where I find comfort in expressing my feelings and hearing the trials and tribulations of other men.

[ciii] I'm telling the next guy, or whoever it is that she may be dating at this current point in time, that he'd better hope that she stays faithful and true because she certainly wasn't to me.

[civ] When did it all happen?

[cv] I never knew the precise time in which I started catching feelings for this girl.

[cvi] This connects with the line above it in terms of "familiarity". A worldwide tour is familiar because it thematically consists of the same concept in terms of structure. It's just in different cities every night.

[cvii] After this girl immediately shut the door on how I felt about her, my feelings were muddled.

[cviii] As fast as I was rejected, I quickly put it behind me. This is becoming a trend isn't it?

[cix] I attempted to change the rules of friendship by coming out to this girl and admitting that I liked her.

[cx] In the summer of July 2013, I received a text message from an old friend which centered around congratulating me on a lot of things I was accomplishing at the time. Ex: Interning at a literary agency; self-releasing my debut crime-fiction novel; owner of my own indie press, also known as *Flowered Concrete*.

[cxi] Her words are important and hold weight to me like stuffing, the bread crumbs that are usually supplied and eaten with Turkey on Thanksgiving Day.

[cxii] Feelings for a person never truly subside, especially if you once had a relationship with them. Instead, you just kind of cast them aside and hide your emotions.

[cxiii] There's no need for tissue since my relationship with this girl panned. We were in fact incredibly young at the time and were just beginning to figure ourselves out as human beings.

[cxiv] Here, I'm saying that if it isn't working she shouldn't put herself in a rough situation. It also ties into the line that follows as a reference to the late lawyer of O.J. Simpson Johnny Cockran and his famous phrase used during O.J.'s infamous murder trial, "If it doesn't fit, you must acquit".

[cxv] We're all searching and constantly seeking for love that is pure. A dove is a white kind of bird and the color "white" in general represents purity in many cultures, especially in America.

[cxvi] I'm patiently waiting for my shot at love.

[cxvii] This girl that I'm talking about in particular has a brother whose name is also Kevin and due to this matter, she calls me Jerry, which is my middle name in order to provide distinction.

[cxviii] Black women in general, whether young or old, are often stereotyped for being crazy, confrontational, loud, aggressive, but in actuality, they're just extremely passionate human beings that are beautiful across the board.

[cxix] A message to young black women as they should carry themselves in a classy, respectful sense. (This includes, dress, speak, manners, etc.)

[cxx] While carrying themselves in a very well presented manner, they should seek gentleman who love and accept them for who they naturally are and respect them to the highest degree.

[cxxi] It was a good Thursday until everything changed for the worst.

[cxxii] The night of Bianca's passing, a mutual friend of ours named James Jones called to inform me of her passing; I was playing NBA 2K13 for the PlayStation 3 when he had made the call.

[cxxiii] After receiving the news, I reflect upon my day at the library and how I felt while I was sitting in there.

[cxxiv] At the time, I was busy working on my second novel, called *"FRANKLY TWISTED"* the sequel to *"Tales of the 23RD PRECINCT"*. Also, I don't ever see my supporters who support my material as fans, I see them as fiction friends.

[cxxv] I really can't explain it but I didn't feel too good internally right around the exact time Bianca passed. I don't know if it was a connection sort-of-thing, but I felt as if I would never write again, I remember putting my pen down in the midst of writing as I felt really sad.

[cxxvi] In a poem I wrote for Bianca called "Love/Hate" I wrote a line that said, "Your love for me, consistent, bold," Therefore, the return of these words consistent and bold are used to reference this poem. In addition, I wanted to give that poem to her and I never got the chance to do so. Now that I look back on it, I definitely regret it.

[cxxvii] Although I wasn't interested in her at a certain point in time, she showed persistence and genuine interest in me for a long time, which is why I eventually caught on.

[cxxviii] We started dating but it was very premature. We both weren't ready for it at the time.

[cxxix] This is basically me posing a set of questions to myself. Was I too mature for her? Was I too mature for my own good?

[cxxx] When I wrote the poem I was twenty-two and she passed at the age of eighteen.

[cxxxi] We first initially started talking when I was twenty and she was sixteen.

[cxxxii] I used to joke around with her and would tell her that she was going to have my kids, in which she would playfully respond, "Never!" The funny thing about it was at the time, I used a joke to cover up how I seriously felt.

[cxxxiii] Everyone who loved her while she was still on earth misses her and hasn't been the same since her departure. Especially her immediate family.

[cxxxiv] After her passing, her siblings took it really hard as they tried to make sense of it all.

[cxxxv] As for me, I struggled to find acceptance in her death. Truth be told, I still do. It was a very dark period for me mentally as I began to ponder upon the duration that is left in my life.

[cxxxvi] I witnessed her mother break down in tears during Sunday service. Literally two or three weeks after the accident.

[cxxxvii] I felt the anxieties and I understood the affliction her mother was suffering through because I initially tried to be so strong during my sister Alexandra's passing until one day I sat in my room, balled up and cried.

[cxxxviii] I wrote this poem on the train while on my way home from an internship; I also had texted Myles that day to give him some comforting words as a brother and good friend would.

[cxxxix] Although Myles never replied and expressed that he had received the text, I just hope he knew that I was being sincere and a good friend that he could certainly depend on.

[cxl] At the time, we were all a part of a youth choir at my church and as I was sitting next to him one Sunday, I caught a

glimpse of Bianca on his iPhone. He was staring at one of her smiling portraits in a focused trance.

[cxli] I consider myself an affectionate and emotional person. I'm saying here that when I express love or grief, especially in her case, my heart literally pours out like a sink would when you raise the sink's lever up to its highest degree.

[cxlii] This life is far from being peachy. There are a lot of unexpected events and tragedies that come along the way.

[cxliii] I'm caught up between the good and bad parts of life. At that time, I was doing well in my personal life, but losing Bianca was also a negative that I had to deal with around that time.

[cxliv] One bad thing is usually followed by another.

[cxlv] No girl has even come close to having my heart the way Bianca did and no one here on out probably ever will.

[cxlvi] I'm a die-hard New Yorker.

[cxlvii] Everything is neat, clean, and perfect.

[cxlviii] They often show New York City's tourists the glitz and glamour of the town, but in reality, they don't even see half of what's really going on. If a tour guide really wanted to show them something, he or she should take them to East Harlem, Brownsville, East New York (Brooklyn), or South Bronx, so that they could see how we're really living.

[cxlix] A florist is a person who sells and arranges plants as well as cut flowers. Here, I use the metaphor of New York being a dirty florist so that one's view of the city from an outsider's standpoint is one that is beautiful. Also, I'm saying that the florist, who could be a politician and a part of the government, is the crutch in terms of the city's infrastructure. A third meaning is with the word florist itself. Florist = Floor

[cl] Since the florist is a dirty professional, he'll do things that you often won't agree with. You're tangled and trapped within the laws that he's set in place for you.

[cli] Here, I'm saying that I'm sinking in the mud because there aren't many options for me and other minorities to make it out of our environments.

[clii] The lily petals are the upper echelon of society that thrive and excel off of the working classes labor and misfortune. Also, lily petals can literally be found on top of a flower which shows their position to the ground. They're definitely not at the bottom.

[cliii] Some daily New York City objects one can often find scattered around the street. Stray cats, boots, cans, rats, all exist in large numbers here.

[cliv] New York City is not shy to pollution due to daily exposure from different gases and toxins.

[clv] New Yorkers are used to these unfortunate stigmas therefore, I'm sarcastically asking, isn't it just mesmerizing and beautiful.

[clvi] I'm trying to be a millionaire. Also a slight reference to Lil' Wayne's *"A Milli"* record from his *Carter III* LP.

[clvii] As I'm trying to make a living, the police force, for whatever reason, singles me out.

[clviii] After being hit and riddled with bullets, I'm fulfilled in a sense that I become everything society expects for a young black man in America; Unsuccessful and dead.

[clix] This line speaks of a boy who becomes a local neighborhood drug dealer and sells coke to make a living for himself and his family. The following line, "it's all so shitty" is basically me saying that, it's sad that he has to resort to this type of hustle in order to get by. It's basically a set up for the young man by society.

[clx] This is another line that speaks of my possible assassination for shedding light on the truth and growing my followers.

[clxi] The pow that is heard in this line is the gunshot by the police. The blood from my body starts to ooze out of me, therefore, I'm left leaking like a woman's breasts after she gives birth to a new born. Pow is also an onomatopoeia (literary device).

[clxii] Youth violence as well as video games often help raise a generation.

[clxiii] It's all about the dollar and the oppressed try to get it by any means necessary. "Auto as the city" is a slight reference to the *Grand Theft Auto Vice City* video game, released in 2002 on Rockstar Games.

[clxiv] The street is stacked with cops (wheat) who are constantly on patrol and surveillance watch.

[clxv] They use and abuse their power to discriminate and racially profile minorities. However, they claim that their job is to serve and protect our communities.

[clxvi] Shockingly, with as much money this country or the state makes due to educational expenses, sports franchises, entertainment, media, and a wide array of other things, we somehow don't have money to aid the working class citizens and the poor.

[clxvii] Every state is almost their own country in terms of the ways they go about setting up their laws.

[clxviii] However, although the states are divided, we ironically get together when it is time to fight in a war for our own beneficial gain.

[clxix] The fact behind the brute sheer force and aggression is that those on top strive to stay on top by all costs and in order to do so, they must crush the weak. Simply put, it's a class thing.

[clxx] I've come as a medical professional to take away all of the pain.

[clxxi] You readers are my patients, as in doctor and patience as in calm state. Double meaning/Homophone

[clxxii] Now that I'm here, I will heal all that are seeking medical attention.

[clxxiii] I will provide a diagnosis that consists of truth and insight.

[clxxiv] A dentist's job is a daily one due to the fact that he probably uses Novocain to numb his patients every day.

[clxxv] Being patient is something that you have to remind yourself to be every day. Also, when one is in the health care profession.

[clxxvi] What does the popular term United States stand for? Also a play on words regarding the U.S. Constitution.

[clxxvii] The stripper on the block is also a prostitute who's obviously selling her goods in exchange for sex. Another socioeconomic issue.

[clxxviii] The teacher is just an authoritative pawn in the grand scheme of things. Temporarily, I am the radical with no political ties to the head figure, who now enters the scene.

[clxxix] Similar to bombs, I as the parachute am falling from out of the sky and invading your personal safe zone.

[clxxx] Here, I'm saying that television is deteriorating the brains of our young children. Also, please, be sure to pay close attention to my use of the words, *"TV"* and *"reality"* at the beginning and end of the line. A word play on so called, *"reality television"*.

[clxxxi] Our children of the next generation are lacking all of the essential tools that will help mold them into unique, healthy, and bright minded individuals due to the influence of television, the internet and mass media at large.

[clxxxii] The star spangled fakes are the American reality television entertainers that influence our children whether we like it or not. I mean, they've so called "got everything". But in actuality, it isn't like that. At least not to our realistic, contemporary modern day society. Moreover, the "parody" reference is used to show the joke of a country we're living in while relating back to showbiz.

[clxxxiii] Trade in the television and video games for books and writing utensils. Have them use their minds as a tool for being innovative and artistic at large.

[clxxxiv] If you give children things such as those mentioned above, they will start to see the world for what it really is as they grow and develop.
[clxxxv] Let's remove our kids from the social networks and get them off of the computer once in a while.

[clxxxvi] Teach them how to be an artist with substance while having true musicianship instead of following trends.
[clxxxvii] Open them up to good music, literature, television, films, etc.
[clxxxviii] I'll teach you all some things that the American public education system fails to mention in depth in regards to Afro-American history.
[clxxxix] 1.) El-Hajj Malik El Shabazz (better known as Malcolm X during his time spent with the Nation of Islam)
    Assassinated February 21st, **1965**
    2.) Dr. Martin Luther King Jr.
    Assassinated April 4th, **1968**
    3.) Huey P. Newton
    Murdered August, 22nd, **1989**

[cxc] Maybe I'm next because of the lyrics I write and what I stand for.
[cxci] I'm real and honest like Tupac Amaru Shakur.
[cxcii] In modern language, I've now acquired a bulls-eye target upon myself.
[cxciii] I've done my job by educating these young black kids that need support and teachings upon being who they are in society.
[cxciv] And as a result, the government conspires and plans to take me out.
[cxcv] They're scared of what I've done and fear a rebellion amongst the people.
[cxcvi] Therefore, in order for them to go back to living their wealthy, daily lives, I must be eliminated.

[cxcvii] Another poem with motifs on social class, they are cooking a feast not meant for me. Also, a slight reference to the seizing of land from the Native Americans.

[cxcviii] They can pretend and bluff all they want but the U.S. Constitution was never written in mind for anyone but the European oppressor. All of the other minority groups were excluded from the genetic make-up of the country. Also, the term *"Native Son"* alludes to the critically-acclaimed novel by Richard Wright of the same name.

[cxcix] People who crave spotlight in the media and want instant fame will do anything for it.

[cc] Once a show cancels or has ended, do you even remember the name of your favorite reality star, better yet, for what skills or attributes that they are considered *"famous"* for?

[cci] The insults and drama are often fruitful in these shows. Such tension and chaos brings ratings.

[ccii] Reality television is fictitious all of the time, but sometimes, you get the disturbing feeling that every day people of American society think that it's real.

[cciii] Here, I'm telling the masses that I'll make what I have to say as plain as I possibly can; Also, "Make It Plain" is a 1994 PBS documentary by William Strickland based on the life of the African-American human rights activist Malcolm X; The meaning behind the phrase was that Malcolm would routinely use it as a sign of him being ready to address his crowd that would regularly attend his weekly speeches at the Audobon Ballroom in Harlem, New York City.

[cciv] What I have to say is as raw as Eddie Murphy's 1987 critically acclaimed stand-up special; Also, Malcolm and Eddie was a 1990's sitcom starring Malcolm Jamal-Warner and Eddie Griffin. I guess you could say that Malcolm's character on the show "Malcolm McGee" was a laid back guy who was very plain and responsible while Eddie's character "Eddie Sherman" was an outlandish fast talker with raw, frenetic energy.

[ccv] As much as we may think we're free, the fact of the matter is that, we're still mentally enslaved. In addition, *"Around My*

Way" (Freedom Ain't Free) is a 2012 single from social-conscious rapper Lupe Fiasco's fourth LP *Food & Liquor 2: The Great American Rap Album Part 1.*

[ccvi] The way you are guaranteed test results from the doctor checking your urination sample is the way you are guaranteed so-called "freedom" or the belief in America.
[ccvii] In all actuality, this isn't what you want in American society.
[ccviii] American kids won't hesitate to express their frustrations in a contemporary society that doesn't necessarily put them first which often leads to them turning to other vices...
[ccix] But as adults, it is our jobs to change the way they think and to influence them to aspire for great things.
[ccx] Adults in this present space of time, can often be more lost as well as conflicted than the kids, therefore, can we blame them for being in the state that we often find themselves in? Also, the line is a play on the popular phrase "lame sitting ducks" in cartoons.
[ccxi] The result of children not having (a) stable parent(s) to look up to is the inevitable cycle of life in poverty stricken urban communities. Also, metaphorically speaking, the kids don't have protection as in contraceptives so they continue to have sex with the possible consequences looming after.
[ccxii] The way in which the public school systems are set up is pure atrocity. Children literally learn reading, writing, arithmetic in elementary, junior high, so on and so on...The only difference between all levels of redundant education is just that it gets a bit harder every step of the way. Also a play on the two words *"school"* and *"trip"*.

[ccxiii] This line focuses on social classes instead of educational ones. It depicts that I'm not just talking about school but also the social ranking of citizens in everyday American society. The one's watching from the bleachers are in fact, the government and the people who rule the country. These people have more wealth and power than any modern day citizen would and are in the bleachers because they are

conducting a surveillance on the working class and everyone else in between (the middle class).

[ccxiv] The media plays a crucial role in modern day society and contemporary lifestyle. Everyone sees their favorite celebrity, athlete, model and wants to look just like them. These are the images that the media tells you are acceptable and what you should be striving for.

[ccxv] The act of boys camping out in line waiting for sneakers is a direct-effect of mass consumption and the materialistic beliefs/images promoted and marketed in corporate America. Therefore, this kid, who is the sole focus of this line at hand, will go out and spend money that he doesn't have in order to purchase this sneaker. Possibly Jordans, or Nike Air Yeezy's.

[ccxvi] The government never ceases to control our youth.

[ccxvii] This boy is now on the corner selling dope to his poor impoverished community. The drugs are probably cheaply made to.

[ccxviii] This kid is now starting to get high off of his own supply.

[ccxix] The kid now comes across his kingpin or possibly a rival drug dealer who shoots him down. Also, here, we learn that the name of the kid is Huey Newton; This poem alludes to the fact that the former co-founder of the Black Panther Party, Huey P. Newton, was gunned down by twenty-four-year-old (at the time) Tyrone Robinson, a Black Guerilla Family member and drug dealer that shot him twice in the face at a West Oakland street corner. Newton's last words were, "You can kill my body, and you can take my life but you can never kill my soul. My soul will live forever!"

[ccxx] I'm tired of what they are saying about us. The socioeconomic plagued peoples.

[ccxxi] Time to revolt, we can't continue to playfully make joking remarks; "B" is slang for homie or considered short for brother in New York City.

ccxxii A message to pimps and men who demean women to stop it. "G" is also another slang word used often in NYC and is short for gangster.

ccxxiii As mentioned before, the world is not pink and the reality of it is what we're living.

ccxxiv A woman that I'm talking to among the masses says she, as well as the people are not used to people giving signs of encouragement.

ccxxv As I'm preaching and spreading the good word, a lot of it happens to go through one ear and out the other. However, this young girl is listening attentively.

ccxxvi Here, I'm saying that she digested everything that I had been trying to teach her and overtime, she was able to recall it all for herself. Also, I mentally fuck her as I pulled back the skin from my scrotum. Therefore, it slipped up like a banana peel.

ccxxvii The teachings that I've passed down to this girl are very appreciated. Also, she digests it slowly and savors it the way a homeless person would every time they are fortunate enough to have a meal.

ccxxviii A majority of my poems are written on the subway. As I was writing this one in particular, I thought of all the things I wanted to say.

ccxxix I'm thinking of all the problems that we're currently facing as a country.

ccxxx Here, I am trying to say that as sure as a Buddhist who is meditating and hovering above the ground, a major factor in terms of conflicts in the United States is due to money. Also, in political terms inflation is another word for money.

ccxxxi What on earth is up with New York City as well as the U.S.A.? We have foreign policies in places in various parts of the world as we poke and prod in affairs that aren't our business.

166

[ccxxxii] It's disturbing that we have so much money for war, sports, entertainment, fortune 500 companies etc. And yet, we have no money for the people who are stranded and starving.

[ccxxxiii] The word "bread" is often used as slang term in New York City to describe money. Also, bread plays off of the fact that homeless people can't afford to eat or buy it. More so, basketball players of the NBA get paid millions of dollars to do what they do and what I'm trying to say here is that if they can get paid to perform and entertain, there should be money to give to the less fortunate.

[ccxxxiv] In Christian based churches, the pastor, reverend or priest often sends around a collection basket for prayer or donation to the church. The purpose of it is something I often question because I personally don't think people should pay for blessings when they can ask God for what it is they seek directly.

[ccxxxv] The social-elite don't visit or help improve impoverished communities. As long as everything is great in their world, then that's all that matters.

[ccxxxvi] We've made strides as a people but yet, we've got a long way to go.

[ccxxxvii] If you're not careful, you may just end up needing CPR (Cardiopulmonary resuscitation) after suffering through police brutality.

[ccxxxviii] Police officers have daily quotas they must meet in order to move up in the ranks and earn their pay. Sometimes the integrity of a cop can be questioned as they will do anything to move up. Sometimes they issue unnecessary ticketing, summons, etc.

[ccxxxix] In New York City, Courtesy, Professionalism, and Respect are the three words labeled on a blue and white police car.

The irony about it though is that some officers use it to their advantage and treat civilians however they see fit.
[ccxl] Our country doesn't know that it is steadily being lied to.
[ccxli] Someone's "Plan A" in life may never come to fruition because Plan B, usually a detractor, hinders them from the process and tells them that they won't be able to achieve it. This act is considered malicious therefore, the word "see" is used as a homophone to the letter *"C"; A,B,C*

[ccxlii] The American government taxes every U.S. citizen and then will use that money to invest in ammunition and weapons of mass destruction for war; We then go to the Middle East in countries such as Iraq, Afghanistan and Syria, and take their oil for our benefits.
[ccxliii] GDP = Gross Domestic Product; GOP = Grand Old Party which is also known as the Republican Party, one of the two major contemporary parties in the United States. Here, I am saying that political factions such as the GOP and market value capita such as the GDP have placed us as Americans, in bad positions to live out our lives.
[ccxliv] There are many major components of history that are non-existent in American textbooks that students use on a daily basis.
[ccxlv] Here, I am offering a suggestion for us as a people to write the story. Our new story about America, its people and every true fact that came before us; I also allude to *It Was Written* the sophomore follow up of hip-hop legend Nas from Queensbridge. The album, like his first was also critically-acclaimed and is considered by many as one of the most important albums to hip-hop and the Mafioso subgenre.
[ccxlvi] A lot of us are prisoners within our own minds. Therefore, it is important that we understand our history and learn from one another, that way we don't end up staying in a constant cycle of repetition.
[ccxlvii] No more time to waste, I'm going to rebel with a rifle or a gun, as Assata Shakur *allegedly* did during the 1973

infamous New Jersey Turnpike Shootout where she *allegedly* killed New Jersey State Trooper Werner Forester while deeply wounding another trooper by the name of James Harper. [ccxlviii] Assata Olugbala Shakur is an African-American activist who was a member of the Black Panther Party as well as Black Liberation Army. After a brief stint in prison for her involvement in the turnpike shootout, Shakur was granted political asylum in Cuba in 1984, after being broken out of prison by members of the BLA; she is also the step aunt of deceased iconic rapper, Tupac Shakur.

[ccxlix] If it wasn't for Black Panthers such as Mutulu Shakur, Tupac's stepdad and also the brother to Assata, I wouldn't be the proud young black man that I am today.

Sidenote: Mutulu is currently serving a life sentence for aiding in his sister's escape from a New Jersey state federal prison.

[ccl] Shout outs and recognition are in order for any young man from the working class that are just trying to survive.

[ccli] Here, I am telling these young guys, to do whatever they can because their chances were never good to begin with. I understand that it is a daily struggle and that they're just trying to get by.

[cclii] The world that I'm currently living in is delusional; A reference to the same line on *Intro* by Long Beach, California rapper, Vince Staples on his June 2013 released mixtape, *"Stolen Youth LP."*

[ccliii] You're either going to fight your way through the street and the decay or remain in poverty as you try to survive.

[ccliv] Teenagers and young adults that get caught up in the cycle of violence are only living the best way they know how. They were born into these environments and given these harsh circumstances.

[cclv] You can't blame them for what society has made them as they have become products of their own environment.

[cclvi] These children growing up are trapped because they have no positive role models to look up to. Also, many of these

young African-American children are off-spring of kids from the crack era. Therefore, it can arguably be said that it was predestined for them to fail. [cclvii] A major ongoing problem in the black American community is the "absentee father". Young mothers are usually forced to play both roles (Mom and Dad) to their children. [cclviii]

In the most dangerous impoverished urban cities of America, kids resort to drug dealing, gang culture, and gun violence as a way to cope within their communities. These environments are so fragmented that children often find themselves in situations that place them on the border line between life and death. [cclix] Take a city such as Chicago for instance, where many neighborhoods such as the Southside and Westside are currently rotting away. These locales have been so brutalized to the point where someone you know is being displayed on the 5pm news, due to the frequency in tragedy. Believe it or not, many of these citizens within and surrounding the communities become desensitized to the violence. [cclx] Bap, bap, bap! If you listen closely as you recite these words, you can hear gunshots ringing out. This is an Onomatopoeia where the word is imitating the natural sound of a gun. [cclxi] The gunshots going off were heard in a school, therefore, a child has snuck a gun into the institution where the narrator's little brother attends. [cclxii] The pigs, (slang for cops) are parked where some kids, (probably handling something illegal) shot at them due to paranoia; Rat-tat-tat-tat is another form of gunshots, also another onomatopoeia. [cclxiii] Kids, most likely the ones who shot at the cops, throw their .9 millimeters in a nearby sewer as a way to hide the evidence just in case they're caught. [cclxiv] The gun toting young men are often just kids who live and die by the thrill of a gun. They want respect in any shape or form and hope that the world, as it is, will recognize their manhood.

[cclxv] The manhood of these kids, however, are put to the test when they are arrested and brought in to testify in court on the stand. After possibly being questioned by a prosecuting attorney, they violate the first street code known to man and snitch on their accomplices/friends.

[cclxvi] The young kid testifying in court has a baby on the way by a girl who is likely as young as him. The word "baby" is used twice here as it:

1.) Shows the relatively young age of this young couple at hand.
2.) Signifies that they are about to have a child.
3.) "Baby" is usually a pet name someone calls their love interest when in a committed relationship.
4.) Points 1, 2, & 3 = triple entendre.

[cclxvii] The irony in this line is that the young man seeking respect and credibility for his rep, (manhood) flees once he learns that he will become a father. Therefore, he is less than a man, literally and figuratively.

[cclxviii] The seed of this unidentified young man turns out to be a girl who has never come across her father.

[cclxix] The girl now grows up to become a teenager, and due to her father's absence, she was never given the love that she needed from a male figure. Therefore, she went seeking for it in all the wrong places.

[cclxx] The girl is now doing one of two things. Due to her living in an impoverished community, she has probably become a prostitute as a way to make ends meet or she is dealing with guys who are players and pimps that constantly demean her.

[cclxxi] First character revealed. Kurt is a boy who grows up alongside this girl in her community that treats her terribly. He starts to have sexual relations with her and abuses her during the process.

[cclxxii] The moment you come off of a crack binge or some type of personal abuse due to drugs and/or alcohol, the only presence that will never let you down is that of God or some

sort of spiritual belief that will be there to uplift you through all of the turmoil.

[cclxxiii] You may think that there is no God, that there is no form of higher power due to all of the constant struggles you've experienced in your life.

[cclxxiv] However, God has a plan for you, as well as everyone. Talk to him, pray, and watch him make a way for you.

[cclxxv] This is me talking, as we are now back to my perspective on things. I'm saying here that these lines are hard because I'm a dick in terms of how I come up with my rhymes (poetry) in my head. Also, the sexual references "come", "dick" and "hard" are all puns intended and make the delivery that much funnier, smoother and clever.

[cclxxvi] As I'm thinking of these lyrics that come to mind, I'm writing them down to show how authentic they are in actuality.

[cclxxvii] My lyrics, no matter if they are presented in fictitious or non-fiction form paint vivid imagery such as a homeless man who starves of hunger and panhandles his way around a city as a means to get by.

[cclxxviii] Three characters are revealed, two of them are even named.

Here, we learn that the name of the battle tested young man is Roy and his girlfriend's name is Ruth. The baby, who grows into the young man she eventually becomes, still isn't named but is in fact the offspring of these two individuals.

[cclxxix] The poem is an exposition that preludes the forthcoming events and introduces all of the story's characters going forward.

You have thus far:

1.) Roy – The teenage father
2.) Ruth – The teenage mother
3.) Asia – Roy & Ruth's offspring
4.) Kurt – The young boy in "Young girl's" generation who starts to date her while physically abusing her at the same time.

5.) Narrator – A young man as well of the ghetto who narrates all five stories of *"Stolen Youth"*.

[cclxxx] An object that's built for war in an impoverished community is often more times than not, a gun. Here, the narrator is suggesting that he possibly carries one due to the tenacious nature of his turbulent community.

[cclxxxi] The narrator owes the landlord some overdue rent. This problem leads to a souring of their relationship and creates hostility between the two.

[cclxxxii] A local gang is trying to recruit this young man and make him "down".

[cclxxxiii] He despises what he sees in the projects that he lives in.

[cclxxxiv] Remember Roy? He was introduced in *Stolen Youth*. Well now he's back on the block and blends in with every other disenfranchised youth within his community.

[cclxxxv] He doesn't understand that he has major responsibilities on his shoulders despite the fact that he is young.

[cclxxxvi] Roy has no choice but to step up and although it isn't made clear whether he does or doesn't, it can be insinuated that he possibly has come to grips with his reality.

[cclxxxvii] As Roy starts to figure things out and possibly begins to piece his life together, he is mercilessly gunned down. It is possible that his dry snitching in the first poem comes back to haunt him.

[cclxxxviii] Once again, Roy's girlfriend Ruth, pops up, and she is sad and depressed due to his death.

[cclxxxix] Ruth is outraged at the fact that Roy would go and get himself killed at a time where she desperately needed him.

[ccxc] Ruth regrets that her baby Asia will never get to meet or experience life with her father.

[ccxci] The story transitions upon the narrator himself. Unlike others, his situation seems to be looking up. The symbolic nature of the sun shining instantly shifts the mood of the poem from dark to optimistic.

[ccxcii] The narrator is ecstatic because his financial aid has come through and he is now able to pursue college cost-free.

[ccxciii] He thinks he gets to further his education and better himself. Well, he's damn right....

[ccxciv] For some reason, he's now feeling a little uncomfortable about his financial aid.

[ccxcv] The narrator is hinting here that his financial aid may not be as legit as we thought it was and that he wants to correct that by either paying it off or not going to school at all. Also, the words "straight" and barbering are also a play on barbershop terms and receiving an actual haircut.

[ccxcvi] He's thinking of all his problems while Guy, a local neighborhood resident, blows his weekly paycheck on the lottery, mind you, Guy doesn't have a lot of money to begin with.

[ccxcvii] Here, the narrator is simply asking why we, as a people, can't work our way from the ground up instead of banking luck on the lottery in which your actual chances of winning are slim to none. Also, "clay" makes pottery and the capitalization of the word GOOD alludes to the rapper, Kanye West's label which uses the acronym G.O.O.D. which stands for Getting Out Our Dreams.

[ccxcviii] The narrator becomes visually sick as he takes a trip to his local corner store.

[ccxcix] He sees a drunkard staggering in front of the corner store who has possibly consumed alcohol throughout the entire day.

[ccc] This wino once had a wife but soon began to abuse her due to his over excessive drinking.

[ccci] This man has become irrelevant and just complains for the hell of it.

[cccii] This narrator aspires to become something due to his future pursuit in higher education and hopes to leave his environment without looking back.

[ccciii] When he ceases to exist, he wants people to remember him for the upstanding citizen that he was.

[ccciv] He hopes that when all is said and done that he has provided light, truth and hope to the youth of tomorrow.

[cccv] After all his motivating and teaching, he hopes that these kids he's mentored will make it out of their neighborhoods and put something positive back within them. Also, he wants them to make it out of their hoodies alive, something seventeen year-old Trayvon Martin was last seen to be wearing before he was gunned down in 2012 by George Zimmerman.

[cccvi] This boy named Kurt had droopy lips which are big and never stay shut. Also, Ma$e was a hip-hop artist who was very popular in the late 1990's. He was best known for rapping alongside label mate, the Notorious B.I.G. and Bad Boy records label owner, Sean "Puffy" Combs.

[cccvii] This kid named Kurt was a hothead and wanted to make a living by any means. He craved the lavish life and wanted it very badly. Also, the word stake is used as a homonym since it sounds like steak. It also ties into the wordplay of the line with both "stake" and "taste" following it shortly after.

[cccviii] Kurt was never in school and could always be found at the local park or nearby mall.

[cccix] One day, he surprisingly showed up to class and so the teacher took the time out to test him.

[cccx] As much as Kurt wished he knew the answers to the questions asked of him whenever he went to class, the fact of the matter was that he didn't know, therefore, he remained silent.

[cccxi] The teacher who we can make an assumption is a female due to the use of the word "doll" tells Kurt that she's had enough and that she will call his parents or guardians to reprimand him.

[cccxii] Kurt verbally retaliated by calling his teacher a "bitch" and that if she's really got a problem with him she should just fight him. This is something that is actually prevalent in today's society, where students in urban public schools lash out at most of the authoritative figures who appear as threats to their credibility. In a sense, Kurt doesn't realize that in actuality she's really trying to help him.

[cccxiii] As the narrator, I'm saying that it hurts me to shed light on such a terrible story of a young misguided man.

[cccxiv] Although he wasn't the most studious or bright, the one thing that Kurt was definitely good at was playing basketball. It was the only thing he ever believed that he was good at.

[cccxv] He put his all into basketball whenever he stepped onto a court, however, there was probably a bunch of people on his level or better that played for an organized school team, therefore, he didn't make it.

[cccxvi] June of 2009 arrives. And it is here we get a shift in the story in terms of climate. The fact that it is now June, it is now warm in terms of temperature.

[cccxvii] By now, many people in his year are starting to graduate and move on to college; and although Kurt made it to his senior year, it was always known that he wasn't going to make it.

[cccxviii] Kurt noticed that some of his fellow classmates were doing great for themselves as they would move on to higher education. However, he wanted to elevate his street cred. And so, he bought a gun and went to a car dealership to get him a ride.

[cccxix] Someone snitched on Kurt and called the cops. Moreover, be sure to take notice of the clever used wordplay in both the words, "squeal" and "pigs". Someone who squeals is considered a snitch, therefore, you have this term setting up the scene.

[cccxx] As Kurt was preparing to retaliate, he had no idea that the cops had marked him from the top of a roof.

[cccxxi] The snipers shoot Kurt and he's lying face down in red (blood).

[cccxxii] After being shot, Kurt now wears a red department of corrections jumpsuit. On the other hand, I as a narrator wished that he would have worn blue, which is usually cap and gown colors for graduation. The juxtaposing of both the colors red and blue also ties into the colors of both the Bloods and Crip gangs.

cccxxiii Kurt hasn't been seen or heard, since his shootout with the police. Therefore, it is likely that he is incarcerated. Also, "pound" is a slang term for prison.

cccxxiv Here, I am trying to refresh everyone's memory as Asia, the daughter of Roy and Ruth is reintroduced. She's also older.

cccxxv Asia's life is crazy and one can say that it has gotten worse from where we last left off with her.

cccxxvi At the age of sixteen, she is no longer a little kid; therefore, she's interested in different things, such as boys now.

cccxxvii She likes this boy in her class named Joey who aspires to be a rapper.

cccxxviii Joey has impregnated Asia with his first child.

cccxxix Asia's mother, Ruth, tells her that it is déjà vu because she herself had Asia at the age of sixteen with Roy, therefore, the cycle continues.

cccxxx We must ask ourselves, "Is Asia really to be blamed for her current dilemma?" It must be stated that her mother is also a lost person. Also, a simile is used to exhibit the misguidance of her upbringing in comparison to six teens and a gun.

cccxxxi Asia never knew what resulted of her father because her mom never told her.

cccxxxii With the absence of a father figure, Asia yearned for love in Joey and thought that she was a recipient of that when they had sex.

cccxxxiii Asia must now come to terms with her pregnancy and wishes that things would go back to how they once were.

cccxxxiv Asia opens up suggestions to her possibly being a young stripper or prostitute; *Twerk* is a term used in modern pop-culture that consists of a woman shaking her rear in seductive fashion.

cccxxxv Here, it is clarified that her line of work is indeed prostitution and if you meet her at the corner, the chances of you fornicating with her are instantaneous.

[cccxxxvi] She's selling her body on the streets while her pimp makes a profit off of her late night escapades.

[cccxxxvii] If Asia doesn't make a certain amount of money for her pimp, she just may be in major sorts of trouble.

[cccxxxviii] She despises this man because he treats her as if she is a piece of dirt.

[cccxxxix] Although she doesn't fancy him, Asia knows that if she doesn't cooperate, the chances of her getting hurt by this pimp are extremely high.

[cccxl] Asia is now being physically beaten as she hasn't reached the number that her boss wanted her to reach. We also find out that the one doing the pimping is Kurt. Most likely this occurred in the past because as we know it, Kurt was placed in prison for attempted grand theft auto. This line also references the boy "Kurt" from the prior story as well as former WWE superstar, Kurt Angle who used to wear purple tights on certain occasions for his matches.

[cccxli] This is my message to girls that are in the same situation as Asia.

[cccxlii] Asia thought if she loved Joey enough he would stay but at the end of the day he's only a sixteen-year-old kid and he wasn't ready to be a father. Sound familiar?

[cccxliii] Asia couldn't get over the fact that he left her. She thought she was special to him.

[cccxliv] The only thing she has been left with is 40 acres, while her mule (unborn child) is in her embryonic sack awaiting birth.

[cccxlv] Asia finally gave birth to her first child. Due to the fact that it happened over the course of the regular school year, she had no other choice but to drop out.

[cccxlvi] Joey was always in control of the situation. He got what he wanted.

[cccxlvii] Asia trusted Joey with all of her heart and really thought he would be there forever.

[cccxlviii] Her trust in him was also as potent as a coin flip in which someone tosses a coin and both parties hope that the end result is in their favor.

[cccxlix] Asia is trapped and feels as if she'll never escape the haunting reality that exists. The poem ends with an allusion to its title. It also references Nas' song *Black Girl Lost* and the Donald Goine's novel of the very same name.

[cccl] The girl Asia had the baby in "Another Black Girl Lost".

[cccli] Asia is all alone because Joey left her to raise the child all by her lonesome. Also, the line, "insane, fuming flames" references an earlier poem in this section called "Neighborhood Watch", where Asia's mother, Ruth, was devastated by Roy's death. Ruth became bitter because Roy had left her all alone to raise their infant daughter. Now it seems as if that feeling has gone from one generation to the next as Asia begins to feel what her mom once felt.

[ccclii] Here, we learn that Asia's baby turned out to be a boy and due to the fact that he's living under a single parent household, he doesn't respect his mother as he should. He takes her for a joke.

[cccliii] There is no doubt that this boy rules his household in contrast to what his mom would like to think. Her face is often as pale as a ghost due to the suffering she endures caused by the stresses of her son's antics. Also, "Ghost" was a popular 1990 film that starred the likes of Whoopi Goldberg, Demi Moore and late actor, Patrick Swayze. In the flick, Swayze's character Sam Wheat is a murdered ghost who tried to save his lover, Molly Jensen, (Demi Moore). Therefore, what I am trying to say is that Asia is horrified as she observes her son become the "Ghost" character in the flesh.

[cccliv] Unsupervised children or kids with no parental guidance are often out late nights and early into the morning. With these young men, it is no different.

[ccclv] A lot of these young men have mothers who are simultaneously playing the role of Dad due to the disappearance and departures of the fathers.

[ccclvi] These boys roll deep in a nine man set kind of like the New York City based hip-hop collective, the Wu-Tang Clan, arguably considered to be the greatest hip-hop group of all time. The members are RZA, GZA, Method Man, Raekwon, Ghostface Killah, Inspectah Deck, U-God, Masta Killa and the late Ol' Dirty Bastard who passed away in 2004.

[ccclvii] Who knows what possibly could have become of these young men if they had fathers present within their lives.

[ccclviii] The boy likes to roll up a blunt and smoke a fat one.

[ccclix] The boy has been making a lot of cash as of late. Drug dealing perhaps. But also, one must remember that, "his cash is flow" leaving open the possibility that he also raps like his absentee father Joey. In addition, his hustle that supplies him with currency is what he's been using as of late to buy his weed.

[ccclx] What makes the situation worse is that his mother Asia gives him money in addition to his hustling ways. The fact that this occurs on the regular shows that people like Asia aren't mentally prepared to have kids at such a young age. Most likely, she was still mentally a child when raising him herself.

[ccclxi] With all the money the boy's been making, we find out he, himself, has a son and doesn't take care of him, which means that he is a dead beat father.

[ccclxii] We learn from previous lines of dialogue that aren't annotated that the boy's name is Rasheed. Rasheed blames the girl who happens to be the mother of his kid for having the child. He blames her for letting it happen as if he didn't have a part in it as well.

[ccclxiii] It was all fun and games for Rasheed and now he bails out on a young struggling mother as well as a kid who will possibly grow up to never know his father.

[ccclxiv] A year goes by and Rasheed's baby boy is now one.

[ccclxv] Rasheed runs away from his manly responsibilities and leaves the young lady and boy to fend for themselves. Also, I use a simile with the word "like" to exhibit how Rasheed stays concealed like illegal guns in automobiles or upon gangsters.

[ccclxvi] Rasheed's son will grow up to be just as violent and mad at the world due to the lacking of a father's presence. Like Rasheed, Asia and Ruth before him, the dead-end cycle continues...

[ccclxvii] If it wasn't for Alexandra Anglade wanting a sibling, I wouldn't be here.

[ccclxviii] I have so much love for my dearly departed sister that I'm vulnerable to cry at any time.

[ccclxix] What I think and how I feel is true.

[ccclxx] Life is as fragile as a breakable object.

[ccclxxi] I struggled through stress and minor depression after receiving word that she had passed away.

[ccclxxii] Metaphorically, I'm saying that I was trying to make sense of the entire situation but somehow, I couldn't.

[ccclxxiii] Although one's heart never fully heals when they lose someone, in due time, they will eventually learn how to cope with the situation.

[ccclxxiv] I proceeded to carry on with living because as we all know, life goes on. Also, the words "pain," "leisure" and "procedure" play on the idea of surgery.

[ccclxxv] I began to take matters into my own hands.

[ccclxxvi] At the age of sixteen, I promised myself that I would make my family proud by becoming something that would allow them to rejoice. I owed it to my sister, family and more importantly, myself...

[ccclxxvii] Life eventually comes to an end but the spirit lives forever.

[ccclxxviii] Prior to my sister passing away, we had gotten into a slight argument but we eventually made up before she left the earth.

[ccclxxix] Often when I'm in a foul mood or feeling sad or depressed, my sister has always been there to pick me up.

[ccclxxx] *Blue's Clues* was a popular television show for kids that aired on Nick Jr. every weekday morning. In the show, Blue, (the dog) and his pal Steve, (owner) always went on adventures searching for clues to solve mysteries/dilemmas.

[ccclxxxi] I don't need to buy love when it comes to my sister because her love is precious and natural.

[ccclxxxii] *"What's on your mind?"* Is the greeting that many come across when plugging in a status on the popular social media network called Facebook. Here, I also use it to ask what may be currently running through my sister's mind.

[ccclxxxiii] Samantha and I often call ourselves twins because we tend to think the same thing sometimes.

[ccclxxxiv] After losing our sister prematurely, it is imperative that both Samantha and I maintain good physical health.

[ccclxxxv] I couldn't imagine journeying through life without her. If I were to lose her, my life would mean nothing. As siblings, we're that close...

[ccclxxxvi] A reference to west coast rapper Snoop Dogg's 1993 single *"Gin and Juice"*.

[ccclxxxvii] I'm rallying for the both of us to accomplish all of the goals we've set out to do in the future.

[ccclxxxviii] A nickname I had during childhood that my father gave me.

[ccclxxxix] *Legends Never Die* is a 2013 album by Long Island emcee, R.A. The Rugged Man. The title is from a song of the same name dedicated to R.A.'s deceased father. I titled this poem after the album because I feel as if my father is alive and well within me.

[cccxc] They go home to the lord.

[cccxci] The soul of a departed person is multiplied when they have more than one child.

[cccxcii] I miss my Dad similar to how Vietnam veterans probably missed their sons during the war.

[cccxciii] A disgraced cop probably misses his firearm in a huge way after being used to it for so long; another way of showing that I miss my Dad.

[cccxciv] Never in a million years would I have thought that I would one day shoulder many responsibilities for my family.

[cccxcv] At the time that I wrote this piece, I was in my last semester as an undergrad at Brooklyn College. I also knew at

the time the career I wanted to pursue shortly after finishing up.

[cccxcvi] After my father passed away, my mother gave every single piece of jewelry that he ever owned to both my sister and I. Actually, she gave one of his chains to my sister and one of them to me. Due to the fact that I inherited what was his, there's no need for me to go out and buy any of my own. [cccxcvii] I feel as if everywhere I go in life, my father is with me. My favorite possession of his that I've inherited is a 10 karat gold ring. I wear it to not only honor him throughout the rest of my life, but to keep him close to me with every move that I make.

[cccxcviii] Anyone who truly knows me certainly knows that I strive for perfection. When my Dad was around he expected nothing less than the best from me and it is because of that attitude that I am now a diligent worker.

[cccxcix] I'm not going to pretend to be some macho tough guy, because I am not. In fact, if I was able to show any kind of affection to my father at this precise moment that I write this, I would love to give him a kiss on the cheek although I know that I can't.

[cd] Similar to rent, my Dad's time here on earth was temporary. That also goes for all of us.

[cdi] I've become the hard working, diligent man that my father once was.

[cdii] Although I grew up in a lower middle class neighborhood, with great surveillance and good parenting from my father, I stayed off of the streets. Also, I play with the word, "Streets" and "Fighter" to exhibit how I was a tough person without literally having to show it. Also, "Street Fighter" for those that don't know, is a 1990's arcade video game classic that still holds significant to many avid gamers who come across it today.

[cdiii] The girl that I was with named Kristina Ortiz abandoned me a little after my Dad's death. Here, I'm personally telling

him that she played me just like the liquor did to his very own life. The word play also ties back into the whole *Street Fighter* reference in the line before it.

[cdiv] I'm continuing in a venting frustration as I tell my Dad what I thought was her love was actually cold and numb like the winter season.

[cdv] Even though I've grown to forgive her for our personal matters and relationship, I can't forget the fact that she neither appeared at my father's wake or funeral to pay her final respects. I felt that if anyone should have been there it was her because my Dad really liked her and treated her with kindness the one and only time that they had met.

[cdvi] Here, I am thanking my Dad for the job well done with me. I'm also letting him know that I understand how hard life is. The latter part of this line which reads "this life is no vacation" directly references an earlier poem within this work called *"Any Means"* (Necessary)

[cdvii] On the weekday, my father prohibited my sister and me from watching television. School nights back then were strictly for homework and reading.

[cdviii] I'm thankful that my Dad would take the PlayStation 2 console that I owned at the time upon every Sunday night before the school week. There is no doubt in my mind that if he didn't, I would have turned out differently.

[cdix] My father was a man who would dress very sharp when he went out to family/friend functions and parties. Therefore, it was only right that he influenced my grooming and stylistic choices as well. Also, I tie in the terms "class" "suits" and "smarts" to show how they're all good "ties". *Tie* such as in the clothing apparel that one usually puts on a buttoned up shirt and tie as in putting all of those assets and attributes together.

[cdx] With my final remark as in *Legends Never Die*, I'm obviously alluding to the title of the poem and how my father's soul will forever live on, not because of me just talking about him, but because the memories we shared live

within my heart and I have fully inherited his best traits that will allow him to live forever.

[cdxi] Every night before bedtime back then, I would pray to God that my maternal grandmother would live forever. I probably was around seven-years-old when I started to think and pray for this. I also hoped for Jesus to come back and resurrect people from death before anything bad could happen to her.

[cdxii] An elixir is a drink used in many fantasy-fictional works that allow people to become immortal. These people after drinking such a potion go on to become supreme beings and live forever.

[cdxiii] I often told myself how cool it would be if I could invent a time portal that would always reverse a possible death that my grandma would eventually endure.

[cdxiv] Along with some of these I just mentioned, I had a plethora of thoughts in terms of cultivating my grandmother's own human existence.

[cdxv] It is well known in my family that my maternal grandmother had her select few favorites, but also, it was a handful of us that truly connected with her the most.

[cdxvi] No woman on this earth, not even the ones who I've adored forever can surpass and eclipse the love and bond I shared with my grandma.

[cdxvii] My grandmother's last name was Bellvue (pronounced Bell-view) and I'm basically saying that she was such a sweet person, that she possibly has her own suite in heaven.

[cdxviii] I saw the pain that my mom was forced to endure after losing her first child. Although, she didn't necessarily cry or express it, her eyes would say it all.

[cdxix] I'm sure that my mom, like the rest of us, couldn't understand or grasp how my sister's passing had happened so fast...

[cdxx] Inexplicable tragedies occur in this world every day, however, we all possibly know someone who's been buried with such unfortunate burden.

[cdxxi] I noticed that with God's love and his guidance my mother's spirit grew each and every day.

[cdxxii] After praying and receiving God's strength, my mother has continued her motherly duties by taking care of my sister and me. I also think that she grew as a mother because of those experiences.

[cdxxiii] There isn't ANYTHING that anyone can say about my mother. The fact that she witnessed the losses of her first child, husband and her very own mother, all in a span of 42 months and is still standing is a sure testament to her faith as well as strength. My mother has made me proud with all that she's done to care for my sister and myself, and I would just like for her to sit and watch me become the man that I am setting out to be…